ENGLISH LANGUAGE SERIES

TITLE NO 8

Speech in the English Novel

Speech in the English Novel

NORMAN PAGE

Associate Professor : University of Alberta

LONGMAN

LONGMAN GROUP LIMITED *LONDON*

Associated companies, branches and representatives throughout the world

© Longman Group Ltd 1973

First published 1973

Cased ISBN 0 582 55036 X
Paper ISBN 0 582 55037 8

Made and printed in Great Britain by
William Clowes & Sons, Limited, London, Beccles and Colchester

To my wife Jean

Foreword

However much the language of fictional narrative could flirt with cadences and structures peculiar to pen and paper, writers have traditionally felt the urge to create dialogue, whether in prose or verse, in something resembling the image of daily speech. The approaches to realism have often been more overt in representing the speech of comic characters:

> Why, Sir John, what do you think, Sir John? do you think I keep thieves in my house? I have searched, I have inquired, so has my husband, man by man, boy by boy, servant by servant: the tithe of a hair was never lost in my house before.

or the speech of dialect characters:

> "Al hayl, Symond, y-faith!
> Hou fares thy faire doghter and thy wyf?"
> "Aleyn, welcome," quod Symkyn, "by my lyf!
> And John also, how now, what do ye heer?"
> "Symond," quod John, "by God, nede has na peer.
> Hym boes serve hymself that has na swayn,
> Or elles he is a fool, as clerkes sayn.
> Oure manciple, I hope he wil be deed,
> Swa werkes ay the wanges in his heed;
> And forthy is I come, and eek Alayn,
> To grynde oure corn and carrie it ham agayn . . ."

But the process has of course extended to fictitious speech more generally. In particular, the novel has over the past two centuries developed so widespread an expectation of such 'realism' in the representation of dialogue and even internal reflection as to obscure the art and convention involved. Yet, as Thomas Hardy wrote in 1891, 'The most devoted apostle of realism, the sheerest naturalist, cannot escape, any more than the withered old gossip over her fire, the exercise of Art in his labour or pleasure of telling a tale'.

While we no longer expect grammarians to go to fictional dialogue for source material in describing natural colloquial language, it is still too little recognized that such dialogue is a deeply interesting object of study in its own right. Professor Norman Page has had his attention firmly fixed upon it for a number of years. His doctoral dissertation at the University of Leeds studied the treatment of speech by that incomparable master of fictional dialogue, Charles Dickens, and he has published a book (1972) on *The Language of Jane Austen*. In the present volume, he ranges over the work of thirty novelists as widely spread in time as Defoe and Salinger, and as regionally and stylistically dispersed as Ivy Compton-Burnett, Ernest Hemingway, and Chinua Achebe. We look at speech reflecting class identity, local identity, and the identity of the individual character. We look at the way the novelist selects from his impressions of the 'reality' around him to suggest the 'reality' of his creation.

This is not the first book in the series concerned with the language of literature nor must it be the last. As English has increasingly come into world-wide use, there has arisen an acute need for more information on the language and the ways in which it is used. The English Language Series seeks to meet this need and to play a part in further stimulating the study and teaching of English by providing up-to-date and scholarly treatments of topics most relevant to present-day English – including its history and traditions, its sound patterns, its grammar, its lexicology, its rich variety in speech and writing, and its standards in Britain, the USA, and the other principal areas where the language is used.

University College London
January 1973

RANDOLPH QUIRK

Preface

Praise or criticism of the dialogue of novels has traditionally been too often based on impression rather than analysis, and easily contented with such shorthand verdicts as the 'brilliance' of Jane Austen's conversation or the 'stilted' quality of much of Sir Walter Scott's. This book sets out to raise some fundamental questions concerning the nature of speech in fiction and its relationship to real-life talk, and to describe the major problems facing the writer of dialogue and some of the ways in which they may be overcome. It also takes a close look at samples of the dialogue of a wide variety of novelists writing in the English language.

My plan has been in the first four chapters to approach the subject of fictional dialogue from the general and theoretical standpoint, and in the fifth and sixth chapters to focus attention on selected novels and novelists. I have not hesitated, however, to draw freely at all times on a wide variety of literary material drawn from several countries and more than two centuries, in the belief that discussion of stylistic questions is likely to be most profitable when it is accompanied by the analysis of specific texts. The use of the novels of Dickens as a major source of exemplification throughout, and the decision to devote a chapter (6) to an extended examination of the role of speech in his work, may serve to impose a rough kind of unity on my eclectic choice of illustrative examples. This prominence given to a single author is explained partly by the fact that my interest in this aspect of language and style originated some years ago in the course of a detailed study of Dickens's work, but mainly by my conviction that he is, among English novelists, the supremely original and versatile exponent of dialogue writing.

Part of Chapter 4 has already appeared in *The Dickensian* and is used here, in a slightly revised form, by kind permission of the editor, Dr Michael Slater. My grateful thanks are also due to Mr John Spencer of the University of Leeds for many valuable suggestions during the earlier stages of my investigation of this topic, and to Professor Randolph Quirk, general editor of the series, for his stimulating reactions to the initial drafts of this book. The extracts from Galt and Alexander quoted in Chapter 3 were brought to my attention by my colleague Dr Raymond Grant.

In all notes and references the place of publication is London unless otherwise indicated.

University of Alberta   N P
January 1973

Contents

Acknowledgments

We are grateful to the following for permission to reproduce copyright material:

Harcourt Brace Jovanovich, Inc, the Author's Literary Estate and The Hogarth Press for an extract from *Mrs Dalloway* by Virginia Woolf.

Chapter 1

Preliminary considerations

'"And what is the use of a book," thought Alice, "without pictures or conversations?"' Both the critic and the common reader have often agreed with Alice in finding the dialogue portions of a work of fiction especially interesting and memorable. The novel-reader is likely to recall with particular vividness the polished exchanges between the characters of Jane Austen or Ivy Compton-Burnett, the dialect writing of Scott and Hardy, the expressive understatements of Hemingway and the brilliant verbosity of Dickens; and, insofar as novels are a source of 'familiar quotations', it is the *speech* of their characters – Oliver Twist asking for more, or Catherine declaring her passion for Heathcliff – that is most often remembered. But whilst there has been much incidental comment on individual books and authors, the verbal texture of dialogue has been little examined, and the fundamental questions of the nature of fictional speech, its role as one of the elements in a novel, and its relationship to other elements and to the speech of real life, have received scant attention.

Most discussion of the nature and methods of fiction has started from the assumption that the novel has as its distinctive task the representation of life in its rich and detailed circumstantiality. We take it for granted that English novelists from Defoe onwards have been concerned to hold up a mirror to reality, and evidence of this assumption is to be found both at the level of formal criticism and in the less sophisticated responses of the reader who regularly uses, as terms of commendation, such epithets as 'realistic', 'convincing', 'credible' and 'true to life'. Yet it is easy to overestimate the extent to which even the most determinedly naturalistic novel does in fact attempt to mirror reality – hasn't it been pointed out that few novels depict their characters eating four meals a day? – and equally easy to overlook or underestimate the importance in this genre of conventions, some of them so familiar as to be unappreciated. To speak of a novel as 'mirroring' life is, indeed, seriously misleading in relation to questions of style, since every work of literature contains in every word a selective and purposive nature that is quite different from the haphazard and arbitrary quality of life itself. Detail in a work of fiction, whether of action, description or speech, and however apparently fortuitous or excessive, can hardly be dismissed as irrelevant, since it belongs to the strictly finite amount of material laid at our disposal by the writer, as distinct from the unselective and virtually unlimited offering made by 'reality'. And since every word of a novel carries a certain weight of significance, it follows that the language in which a novel is composed is likely to have a density and meaningfulness, and will bear a degree of scrutiny, that is not always granted to, or expected from, the discourse of everyday life. The point has been well made by Mark Schorer:

> As for the resources of language, these, somehow, we almost never think of as part of the technique of fiction – language as used to create a certain texture and tone which in themselves state and define themes and meanings; or language, the counters of our ordinary speech, as forced, through conscious manipulation, into all those larger meanings which our ordinary speech almost never intends.[1]

If the novelist's aim is to create the illusion of contact with 'life', he is likely to achieve it by the adoption of certain conventions – not least notably where the presentation of speech is concerned – which assist in producing that willing suspension of disbelief which consitutes the novel-reader's faith. The history of the novel is partly the history of the adoption and development of these conventions. One of the most prominent of them is the process of selection, by which a measure of artistic concentration is produced which the simple reproduction of the detail of everyday life would too readily dissipate. On these grounds, one must question many traditional descriptions of the novel which stress the directly imitative nature of fiction. A comment in a standard guide will serve as a convenient example. 'Like any other artist', writes Walter Allen, 'the novelist is a maker. He is making an imitation, an imitation of the life of man on earth. He is making, it might be said, a working model of life as he sees and feels it.'[2] The analogy of a working model, which implies the accurate reproduction of the parts in spite of a reduction in scale, appears to ignore both the essentially different natures of literature and life, and the ineluctable fact that every novelist must choose to ignore most of what he 'sees and feels'.

If the novel imitates life, then, this must be taken as an account of its effect rather than of its methods; and novelists have discovered that, paradoxically, the quality of life can be most successfully evoked by exploiting the conventions that the development of prose fiction has made available to them, rather than by a too scrupulously faithful adherence to actuality.

In the creation of illusion in a work of fiction, the presentation of speech has a distinctive role, for it is in this element that the closest 'imitation of reality' is likely to appear to take place, if only because the author's presence appears (and it is again, of course, no more than an appearance) to be least obtrusive. In the extreme case of the first-person narrative, or monologue, the author has apparently disappeared entirely (or, to put it another way, has 'become' one of his own characters). Narrative, description, comment – these are familiar literary modes; but dialogue surrounds us throughout life, both outside and inside novels. Not, of course, that speech in a novel can usefully be considered in complete isolation from other elements. Henry James makes this point plainly enough when he speaks of the different elements in a novel as 'melting into each other at every breath, and being intimately associated parts of one general effort of expression'.[3] It is obvious that dialogue will often serve the purpose of advancing simultaneously one or more of these other elements: that is, a given stretch of text consisting mainly or entirely of dialogue may nevertheless help to develop 'plot' and enrich the reader's understanding of 'character' and 'background', whilst at the same time possessing a distinctive and intrinsic interest which no other manner of presentation could provide. (See, for a convenient instance, the dialogue between Pip and Herbert Pocket in Chapter 22 of Dickens's *Great Expectations*.) Provided this is borne in mind, however, the problems of speech-presentation are of a sufficiently distinct kind to make discussion of them meaningful.

In reading fictional dialogue we may well have the illusion of 'listening' to the conversation of those we know well (though some dialogues, of course, have a purpose other than persuading the reader of their probability). What is the nature of the written speech which performs this mimetic role? A familiar kind of tribute to such writing is to praise it for its closeness to real speech. We are told, for instance, that 'dialogue . . . consistently echoes the accepted speech of the day', that 'there is no line of dialogue from a novel that could not easily be imagined proceeding from the mouth of an actual person'; and, of a modern novel, that 'the dialogues . . . could not reproduce actual speech more faithfully, and more unselectively, if they had been transcribed from a tape-recorder'.[4] These are striking claims, from impressive sources. But it seems probable that the whole concept of realism as applied to fictional speech is often based on an inadequate or inaccurate notion of what spontaneous speech is really like.

We still know too little about its structural and other features, and about the distinguishing characteristics of its multitudinous varieties; and what is known has not always been readily accessible to critics whose preoccupations are literary rather than linguistic. The study of speech in fiction has suffered, therefore, from a double disadvantage: in addition to the general disregard until quite recently of the language of fiction as a proper, or at least a feasible, field for investigation, there has been widespread ignorance of the detailed anatomy of actual speech, some knowledge of which makes possible a sense of the extent to which fictional dialogue is conventional and non-realistic. This ignorance has not, however, prevented the spoken language from being frequently invoked as a norm against which dialogue may be judged. Even where present-day literature is concerned, and where we ought to be in a peculiarly strong position to perceive the essential differences, there has been a common tendency to exaggerate the resemblance of written dialogue, or the written language in general, to everyday speech. A notable example is J. D. Salinger's *Catcher in the Rye* (1951), which has been widely praised for its skilful reproduction of an 'authentic' teenage idiom, but of which its author wrote that 'he would never think of using what people actually say for dialogue in his novels. He insisted that nobody would believe it'.[5] Other instances confirm that a persuasive effect of colloquialism may be revealed, on analysis, to depend upon only a very limited and selective observance of the features of actual speech. The first-person narrative of Alan Sillitoe's short story 'The Ragman's Daughter' is a monologue which clearly seeks to suggest the tone and idioms of spontaneous speech. The opening lines are representative:

> I was walking home with an empty suitcase one night, an up-to-date pigskin zip job I was fetching back from a pal who thought he'd borrowed it for good, and two plain-clothed coppers stopped me. They questioned me for twenty minutes, then gave up and let me go. While they had been talking to me, a smash-and-grab had taken place around the corner, and ten thousand nicker had vanished into the wide open spaces of somebody who needed it.
>
> That's life. I was lucky my suitcase had nothing but air in it. Sometimes I walk out with a box of butter and cheese from the warehouse I work at, but for once that no-good God was on my side – trying to make up for the times he's stabbed me in the back maybe. But if the coppers had had a word with me a few nights later they'd have found me loaded with high-class provision snap . . .
>
> [*The Ragman's Daughter*, 1963, 7]

The language is not only unmistakably colloquial, but reasonably specific, apparently belonging to a working-class speaker, probably urban and male, of the mid-twentieth century. After a single rapid reading, most readers might feel that the writer's purpose had been accomplished – as, indeed, it has, if his aim is merely to give a general impression of a familiar variety of lower-class speech, racy, slangy, confident, openly contemptuous of conventions of 'correct' English, and strictly limited in its capacity for description or reflection. As an accurate reproduction of such speech, however, it obviously neither goes nor is intended to go very far. To say that a scholar of the future interested in the twentieth-century demotic will not find it very informative is, of course, a description rather than a criticism, for its purpose is to create a certain impression: the point being stressed at the moment is that, as already suggested, this impression is most successfully created by a very partial and restrained use of the features of living speech. It relies, for example, almost entirely on a small and easily definable category of lexical items to achieve its distinctive flavour: such words as *coppers, nicker, no-good, snap* are within the province of the dictionary or thesaurus of slang, and particularly those sections of such a work which deal with the professional dialect of the criminal classes. It may not be going too far to say that such a style could have been devised solely with the aid of reference-books, rather than by going out into the market-place with notebook and pencil, or by a long-standing personal acquaintance with this form of speech. Vocabulary apart, there are only occasional attempts to suggest a style that has little in common with formal written English and with standard educated speech – in, for example, the use of *that* in 'that no-good God', and in the placing of *maybe* at the end of the same sentence. But of the syntactical patterns which are characteristic of informal speech there is hardly a trace. The third sentence is, with its carefully-positioned subordinate clauses, as typical of traditional written prose in its structure as any sentence in a *Times* leader. Compare, shortly after the passage quoted, the following: 'We once saw, after checking the lists, that there was one cheese extra, so decided to share it out between a dozen of us and take it home to our wives and families'. It is not thus that warehouse-employees, or university professors for that matter, habitually speak. For all its superficially colloquial character, Sillitoe's prose is in fact a long way from speech, and only avoids a commonplace flatness by the use of words and phrases not usually encountered in written prose. Inevitably, such a style constantly trembles on the verge of cliché ('wide open spaces', 'stabbed me in the back'); perhaps the most genuinely idiomatic phrase in the passage is 'an up-to-date pigskin zip job', with its extensive premodification of the head word *job*, involving *two* adjunct nouns ('*pigskin zip* job').

Even with contemporary writing, then, we need to exercise extreme caution in referring to a given style as 'colloquial' or 'speech-based': such terms are not without meaning, but their meaning is little more than relative (Sillitoe is more colloquial than, say, Lawrence Durrell, but his prose is still remote from speech). With any text that is more than one or two generations old, such comparisons must be even more tentative, since we cannot reasonably claim to compare a written style with a spoken language of which, in the nature of things, we can have only a very imperfect knowledge. But for various reasons it seems overwhelmingly likely that no dialogue in novel or play will consist merely, or even mainly, of an accurate transcript of spontaneous speech. It is important to insist at this point that there is an inevitable gap – wider or narrower at different times, but never disappearing entirely – between speech, especially in informal situations, and even the most 'realistic' dialogue in a work of literature.

There are at least three important reasons why this should be so. In the first place, the normal characteristics of the spoken language, even in its 'standard' variety, though they are perfectly tolerable in the *spoken* form, would be quite unacceptable in the *written* medium of the novel. This much is obvious as soon as one looks at an accurate transcript of almost any spontaneous exchange, with its hesitations and repetitions, its 'silence fillers', 'intimacy signals' and 'normal errors', its grammatical inconsistencies and incompleteness and frequent changes of direction. These differences are, given the respective natures of the spoken and written media, hardly a matter for surprise. For obvious reasons, the speaker who is sending his unrehearsed words forth into the air, to be picked up by a possibly inattentive listener, is likely to use language very differently from the writer who is able to express his meaning with the advantages of premeditation and revision, and who knows that he can be read as slowly and as often as his reader chooses. Observing that 'We are unaccustomed to seeing the actual events of speech in written form', Randolph Quirk has quoted, instructively as well as entertainingly, from transcripts of the recorded speech of university graduates in English. The following is a typical sample:

> he – seemed of course he had that kind of n er I I'm er I I er I I er er are you northern by any chance I was going to say that kind of northern – er – scepticism or at least questioning mind – which er – but of course he

would mislead you with that he er he gave you the impression that he only er you know he gave you the impression that he was – sceptical and at times sceptical and nothing else – . . .[6]

Such a passage offers indisputably 'real' speech, but no novelist is likely to inflict this kind of thing on his readers in the name of dialogue. (Perhaps fortunately, few novelists are aware that spontaneous speech can be, and often is, of this kind.) The fact that we respond with surprise when we meet it in the written form – for which, of course, it was never intended – is evidence that the experience is an unfamiliar one, though we may listen to and also utter something very similar every day of our lives. Most novelists silently decline to make any attempt to reproduce these features of the spoken language in anything like their fullness, though they may incorporate in their dialogue a small and judicious *selection* of such features, or may explicitly admit that the author (or narrator) has exercised his discretion in omitting what might be tedious and obscure. Thus, the narrator in a recent novel confesses that he has, in the interests of lucidity, chosen to 'edit' the 'original' speech of his characters in the process of presenting it to the reader:

> There was not much dinner conversation; eating was heavy and methodical and serious, and it would be just as well to record all that was said in one swoop, rather than indicate the sentences lost in the passing of food, the words gurgled into mouthfuls, the syntax chopped and forgotten in heapings, spillings, and gorgings.
>
> [Philip Roth, *Goodbye Columbus*, 1959]

Language 'chopped' and 'gurgled' in this way is likely to be better described than precisely rendered. The obscurities of dialect can also tempt the writer to this kind of act of renunciation, as when Wilkie Collins makes one of his narrators in *The Moonstone* observe, apropos of a dialect speaker,

> (Nota bene – I translate Mrs Yolland out of the Yorkshire language into the English language. When I tell you that the all-accomplished Cuff was every now and then puzzled to understand her until I helped him, you will draw your own conclusions as to what *your* state of mind would be if I reported her in her native tongue.)

Some more determined efforts to represent 'the Yorkshire language' *within* the dialogue will be considered in a later chapter. But, for both writer and reader, there are certain obvious advantages (as well as equally

obvious limitations) in this once-and-for-all method of indicating speech
characteristics. The alternative to such a decision – whether acknowledged
or, as is more often the case, unacknowledged – is a kind of dialogue that is
not without an interest and expressiveness of its own, but which runs the
risk of distracting attention from what is said to the manner of saying it,
as well as damaging the rhythm of an episode by demanding an exceptionally slow and careful reading.

The novelist, then, is apt to find himself with divided loyalties; and in
practice the attempt to represent speech at all fully, literally and accurately
will usually take second place in favour of the requirements of his overall
fictional purposes. Hardy conceded this when he maintained that the first
obligation of the writer who seeks to render dialect speech is to the novel
as a work of literature, rather than to phonetic or other kinds of verbal
precision: as he wrote, his own purpose was 'to show mainly the character of the speakers, and only to give a general idea of their linguistic
peculiarities'.[7]

Secondly, the spoken word in real life (and, to some extent, on the
stage) derives much of its significance from the context of situation, the
relation of language to all those extra-linguistic features which, in a novel,
must be rendered consciously and explicitly, and can only be rendered
partially, by linguistic means. That is to say, whereas a speaker enjoys and
exploits, even if unconsciously, the 'given' elements in a situation in
which he is using language, a writer putting words into the mouth of a
character must select and draw attention to the particular features of the
fictional situation which are at the moment relevant. After all, in a real-
life situation speaker and listener are normally in the same place at the
same time. (Such special cases as telephone conversations and radio broad-
casts are of considerable interest, as involving distinctive linguistic features
by way of compensation for the physical separation of the participants,
but need not detain us here.) On the other hand, the novelist, although he
may well desire to create a sense of the here and now by means of his dialogue, has no shared context available which he can take for granted, but
must produce it verbally within the text of his novel. For this reason among
others, fictional dialogue is likely to be more heavily burdened with informative and suggestive detail than the speech of everyday life, though
this burden is also shared by the non-dialogue elements. This greater
explicitness and spotlighting of particular contextual elements may deprive
fictional dialogue of some of the subtlety and meaningful ambiguity of an
actual speech situation, but it guarantees by way of compensation a clarity
and precision that help to make 'literary' dialogue essentially different

from everyday talk – more self-explanatory and self-contained, sharper and surer in its effects, and therefore more memorable.

Thirdly, in spoken dialogue, whether in life or in a performed play, a good deal of information is carried by the phonological component, which the established conventions of the written language are only very imperfectly equipped to convey. This much has often been confessed by those who have tried the experiment of indicating, for example, features of pronunciation with any real attempt at fullness or accuracy. The best-known example is perhaps Shaw's abandonment of the presentation of Eliza Doolittle's Cockney in *Pygmalion*, after only three speeches. Further-more, such devices as punctuation, though not without their expressive uses, are only a relatively crude and sometimes ambiguous attempt to convey such meaningful features of the spoken language as pause, stress, tempo, volume and intonation. The fact remains that the twenty-six letters of our alphabet, however ingeniously combined and supplemented by other graphological indications, can scarcely begin to represent the in-finite variety and subtlety of speech. All this, however, has not deterred writers from doing their best with the means at their disposal to enable written language to suggest the phonetic qualities of speech. Variant spellings, for instance, have been widely employed by novelists from the eighteenth century onwards, to provide signals of non-standard pro-nunciations. With less trouble, necessary guidance to the reader has been given through the use of direct statement outside the dialogue, if only by some such simple formula as 'he murmured' or 'she said reproachfully'. Internal and external indications may be used in combination, as by the contemporary novelist who wrote the following:

"Whatsh all thish here?... Whatsh going on?" Edwin noted the wet palatalisation of both the alveolar fricative phonemes.
[Anthony Burgess, *The Doctor is Sick*, 1960]

These are only partial solutions, however. Dialogue in a novel, which is written to be read, usually silently, will necessarily involve a redistribution of balance whereby the words themselves may carry as much as possible of that proportion of the total meaning which, in the spoken language, is conveyed by phonological features. (This is to assume for the moment that the writer is not wholly indifferent to the peculiar and distinctive nature of speech and the problems of representing it on paper.) Dialogue is likely, therefore, to be fuller and more explicit in its statements, lacking the suggestions and implications, the undertones and overtones, which may constitute a significant dimension of even the most trivial utterances.

Mark Twain observed in one of his letters that 'The moment "talk" is put into print you recognize that it is not what it was when you heard it; you perceive that an immense something has disappeared from it.'[8] The novelist who aims at producing, through his different medium, a sense of the spoken language is concerned with recapturing this 'immense something', and because he is never likely to be wholly successful it does not follow that his efforts will not repay careful study.

This, then, is the central dilemma of the writer of dialogue: he seeks to create by the use of one medium the effect of language used in another, and if there is a means by which this can be accomplished, however incompletely, it is certainly not by the slavish reproduction of the features of actual speech. As another nineteenth-century novelist, R. L. Stevenson, insists (in a letter to Henry James), people 'think that striking situations, or good dialogue, are got by studying life; they will not rise to understand that they are prepared by deliberate artifice and set off by painful suppression'.[9] For most novelists, the acceptable solution has generally been (unless, of course, all attempt at verisimilitude has been renounced) to create or adapt, and observe, consciously or otherwise, a set of conventions which will vary in nature and importance from novel to novel. Although real speech is often wasteful and disorganized, he will exercise a much stricter verbal economy, even when his purpose is to create an impression of loquacity or tedium. No real-life bore utters speech as purposeful and informative as Miss Bates in *Emma*, and no gin-sodden old woman ever held forth in the disciplined rhetoric of Dickens's Mrs Gamp. This heavier loading of intention, and more regular form and patterning, help the writer to achieve those 'larger meanings' which Schorer has already been quoted as finding in fictional dialogue. Such dialogue is often characterized by a greater density of features which may well be found to appear, only much more thinly distributed, in real speech; and the result will in consequence sometimes strike the critical reader as containing elements of exaggeration, though this exaggeration may be arguably deliberate and necessary.

At the same time, however, the need to give an *impression* of realism remains; and this is likely to be accomplished by the establishment of a delicate balance between the use of some of the observed features of actual speech and the interposing of a more or less elaborate code of stylistic conventions. Hemingway's dialogue has been praised for giving 'an illusion of reality that reality itself would not give',[10] and the paradox neatly sums up the element of art concealing art in much so-called realistic dialogue. Such praise is a tribute to the success with which the writer has performed this balancing-act: a little more 'convention', and the dialogue would be rejected as 'literary' and 'artificial'; a little less, and it would lose its sharpness and sureness, with authenticity a poor compensation for the blurring of the total effect. An appreciation of this necessary compromise seems essential to an understanding of the true nature of fictional dialogue, and one must therefore disagree with those who overestimate the extent to which dialogue is based on actual speech, as one must also with the editor of the *Oxford Book of English Talk*, when he suggests that 'In reading a novel we generally know when we are getting the real thing, and when we are being fobbed off with a piece of literary dialogue'.[11] This antithesis between 'the real thing' and 'literary dialogue' in a pejorative sense is surely misleading. All dialogue in novels, short stories and plays is literary dialogue, though more obviously so in some cases than in others; and most readers are so conditioned by long experience of reading and listening to fictional and dramatic dialogue of many kinds that they would probably not recognize 'the real thing' if they saw or heard it, and would not much care for it in any case. The choice is not the simple one between 'the real thing' – transcribed as it were from a tape-recorder concealed under the table – and the spurious article which offends us by its obvious remoteness from natural speech (though the latter certainly exists). What is involved is, rather, the nicely-calculated question of the kind and degree of convention adopted, and its relationship to the tone and mode of the novel as a whole. Thus the somewhat extreme examples from *Jane Eyre* which Sutherland quotes in support of his argument illustrate a failure of calculation on Charlotte Brontë's part (not the only one in that novel), perhaps stemming ultimately from a basic uncertainty whether she was writing in a realistic or a non-realistic genre. If dialogue is too close to actual speech – which, as *Hansard* and other publications repeatedly illustrate, so often strikes one in the written form as flat, stale and unprofitable – the reader is likely to become weary or irritated. The dialogue technique will fail, that is, to the extent that it calls attention to itself. If, on the other hand, it is too remote from actual speech, the reader's sense of reality may be offended. A Wessex milkmaid need not – *should* not – talk precisely like a rustic, but still less must she sound like a duchess or a schoolmistress. (This is to leave out of account that important category of dialogue which, often for comic or satiric purposes, makes no attempt to persuade the reader of its credibility.)

The importance of dialogue in relation to other elements in a work of fiction will obviously vary a good deal from one novel to another, and between different parts of the same novel. For the novelist, unlike the dramatist, is at liberty to combine speech with narration, description and commentary in proportions that may constantly be varied; and this liberty involves the responsibility of selecting at many points the most appropriate mode or combination of modes for a particular passage, scene or episode. One of the by-products of the combination of dialogue with other elements is the stylistic variety which comes from the contrasts thus brought into play. As well as asking of any novel what use it makes of speech (in any of the forms in which this may be presented), we may enquire what stylistic relationships exist between dialogue and non-dialogue passages. The opening of a novel by a contemporary writer whose interest in speech and its presentation is far-ranging will serve to illustrate this point. Muriel Spark is a poet and dramatist as well as a novelist; one of her books, in which short stories appear by the side of scripts written for radio broadcasting, is titled *Voices at Play* (1961), and the Author's Note to that volume confesses, in relation to the 'ear-pieces' it contains, that the author 'turned my mind into a wireless set and let the characters play on my ear' – an observation that might perhaps, apart from the anachronism, have been made by Jane Austen or Dickens. *Memento Mori* (1959) begins with a telephone message, 'Remember you must die', and her first novel, *The Comforters* (1957), of which the following passage is the opening, is partly concerned with auditory hallucinations:

On the first day of his holiday Laurence Manders woke to hear his grandmother's voice below.

"I'll have a large wholemeal. I've got my grandson stopping for a week, who's on the BBC. That's my daughter's boy, Lady Manders. He won't eat white bread, one of his fads."

Laurence shouted from the window, "Grandmother, I adore white bread and I have no fads."

She puckered and beamed up at him.

"Shouting from the window," she said to the baker.

"You woke me up," Laurence said.

"My grandson," she told the baker. "A large wholemeal, and don't forget to call on Wednesday."

Laurence looked at himself in the glass. "I must get up," he said, getting back into bed. He gave himself seven minutes.

He followed his grandmother's movements from the sounds which came clearly through the worn cottage floorboards. At seventy-eight Louisa Jepp did everything very slowly but with extreme attention, as some do when they know they are slightly drunk. Laurence heard a clink and a pause, a tinkle and a pause, breakfast being laid. Her footsteps clicked like a clock that is running down as she moved between the scullery and the little hot kitchen; she refused to shuffle.

Taken as a whole, this passage is likely to strike the reader as admirably brisk and economical in its use of language: information and suggestion are conveyed with unobtrusive ease. Passing beyond impressions, closer inspection reveals a marked difference between the dialogue and narrative styles, and a further difference, less marked but not imaginary, between the language of the two speakers. The narrator uses sentences structured according to traditional patterns, with both coordination and subordination; the young man's speeches, though brief, are cast in sentences which are grammatically complete in accordance with the norms of written prose (as befits one who is 'on the BBC'); but the old woman's speeches follow conventions significantly different from those of written prose. Typical of these last are such units as:

"Shouting from the window."
"My grandson."
"A large wholemeal . . ."

These are complete in every sense except that of traditional prescriptive grammar: each of them offers the expression of an idea that is readily grasped, what is lacking in explicit statement being supplied by the context of situation; thus the baker is no more puzzled by the third example than are real-life bakers by similar expressions used every day. The usual concept of the sentence, as defined in relation to written prose, is likely to exclude such units, yet they can scarcely be stigmatized as incorrect or incomplete: their meaning may not be profound, but it is perfectly clear. Some of the old woman's other structures defy the normal requirements of 'correct' English in a different way, and recall those offered to schoolboys for 'improvement':

"I've got my grandson stopping for a week, who's on the BBC."
"That's my daughter's boy, Lady Manders."
"He won't eat white bread, one of his fads."

The first two of these appear to relate the words following the comma to a noun that common sense tells us is not the one in question. The third requires us to take 'one of his fads' as a separate unit similar to those already quoted, complete in every respect except that of traditional grammar. Such patterns, though distinctly original in fictional dialogue, are widely used and accepted in everyday speech. Here they function not as linguistic oddities but as modes of expression entirely congruous with the offhand manner of Mrs Jepp, whose abrupt and dismissive remarks are part of her character and of the privilege accorded to the old to indulge their eccentricities.

With the rejection to a substantial extent of normal prose structures goes a retreat from the ordered logicality of written language. The old woman is not afraid of repeating herself, and her responses to her grandson's remarks are in no sense replies:

> "You woke me up," Laurence said.
> "My grandson," she told the baker . . .

Nor is the colloquial quality confined to the syntax or the relationship between sentences, for the lexical features of the dialogue and narrative elements exhibit certain contrasts. The colloquialisms of the former ('fads', 'adore', 'on the BBC') differ sharply from the more 'literary' language of the latter, which is to say that words such as 'puckered' and phrases such as 'the worn cottage floorboards' and 'with extreme attention' would be unlikely to occur in informal speech (except perhaps facetiously). Not only do the two alternating styles (to overlook for a moment the differences between the idiolects of various speakers) provide variety: the narrative style, by observing with reasonable faithfulness the conventions of written prose, forms a 'neutral' background against which the eccentricities of the dialogue – only of course eccentricities by the irrelevant standards of the written language – can be more clearly perceived. One implication of this is that the novelist who decides to use a speech-based style as his *narrative* medium (in, for example, such first-person narratives as J. D. Salinger's *Catcher in the Rye* and P. Roth's *Portnoy's Complaint*) is likely to sacrifice the advantages of the variety and contrast described, even if he does not also run into the more positive danger of ultimate stylistic monotony. Dickens's ingenious and effective solution to this problem in *Bleak House* will be discussed later. Salinger and Roth, while undeniably creating idioms of considerable power and expressiveness, are capable of inducing a sense of lassitude in the reader from the very lack of stylistic contrast.

Although dialogue will often serve to advance plot, and in certain writers (Jane Austen and Ivy Compton-Burnett come quickly to mind) will carry a large share of this function, its more customary role is to contribute to the presentation and development of character; and here its strength lies in its being more direct and dramatic than authorial exposition. We know Squire Western and Mrs Gamp largely by the words they utter, and their individual modes of expression, rather than through what we are told of them by Fielding and Dickens through narrative or comment. For the sake of both clarity and variety, many writers will seek to differentiate between the speech of at any rate their major characters; thus speech becomes at the same time a badge of identity and a means of enriching the reader's awareness of a given character's individuality. The practical advantages of some degree of differentiation are obvious, particularly in a thickly-populated novel (and, *a fortiori*, one published over a period of time). *Nicholas Nickleby*, for instance, contains nearly 120 speaking parts, and the fact that we recognize the familiar idiolects of Squeers or Mantalini on their successive and in some cases widely-spaced appearances helps to give unity to what might otherwise be a diffuse novel with a good chance of leaving the reader hopelessly bewildered. Indeed, the experience of repeatedly encountering well-known 'voices' is one of the ways in which a sense of the distinctive world of a novel is acquired. Nor is the method confined to any one period: to select a handful of examples at random, Parson Adams and Joseph Andrews in Fielding's novel, Miss Bates and Mrs Elton in Jane Austen's *Emma*, Mr Brocklehurst, St John Rivers and Mr Rochester in Charlotte Brontë's *Jane Eyre*, Henchard and Farfrae in Hardy's *The Mayor of Casterbridge*, Piggy and Ralph in Golding's *Lord of the Flies*, are all individualized substantially, and in some instances almost entirely, through their speech.

Such differentiation may take a number of forms or combinations of forms, and without anticipating the fuller discussion of the question in subsequent chapters, these may at this stage be briefly indicated. We identify characters in fiction – as to some extent we do people in real life – by the personal and group characteristics they display; and among these, in any acquaintance that goes beyond the merely superficial or transitory, speech-characteristics are likely to have special importance. Lest I should appear to be falling into the error already castigated, of relating fictional speech too closely to actual discourse, let it be quickly added that what is intensively and extensively exploited in a novel may exist only to a limited degree in life. Just as the dramatic soliloquy is a highly-developed and conventionalized extension of the indisputable fact that many people talk to themselves, character-individuation through dialogue is based on the observable facts of life but often goes a good deal further than most of the examples that life is apt to provide. But it needs no exceptional verbal awareness to associate living individuals with minor mannerisms of speech – an unusual fondness for particular words and phrases, idiosyncratic pronunciations, and so forth: most of us could without difficulty compile a list of such features in the speech of those we know well, including ourselves. With those who speak a good deal in public, such as teachers and preachers, professors and politicians, salesmen and disc-jockeys, such features are often even more apparent, and it is a matter of common experience that certain callings (clergyman, waiter, sports commentator, street-market vendor, etc) tend to encourage the development of highly idiosyncratic speech, if only during business hours. Many novelists have simply based upon these well-known facts a useful set of conventions, which help both to establish a character's identity and to facilitate subsequent recognition. Underlying all these devices is the assumption – not altogether, as has been suggested, a matter of convention – that what a man is and does leaves its mark on his speech. Syntactical features may therefore be seen as expressing timidity, impetuosity or pomposity; particular lexical qualities may convey simplicity, duplicity or pedantry – the list might be lengthened indefinitely. And as, in life, we constantly make judgments (or misjudgments) about character and background on the basis of speech-characteristics, the novelist invites us to do this more confidently, since we know that the evidence has been 'planted' in the dialogue with a set purpose.

If we refer to individual modes of speech as *idiolects*, the term *dialects* may conveniently be used to describe characteristics common to a group – not only a group regionally defined but, using the term in its wider sense, including social and occupational groups. Here again, dialogue which makes use of various kinds of dialect is not based solely on a literary convention, life providing plenty of parallels; but, as always, the principles of selection and concentration are generally at work to give fictional dialogue a quality quite different from that of real speech. Dialects of all kinds are discussed in Chapter 3.

It will be helpful at this point to lay side by side several short passages of fictional speech, which between them exemplify, and will serve to test the validity of, many of the points already made in this chapter:

1 "Why did he kill himself, Daddy?"
   "I don't know, Nick. He couldn't stand things, I guess."
   "Do many men kill themselves, Daddy?"
   "Not very many, Nick."
   "Do many women?"
   "Hardly ever."
   "Don't they ever?"
   "Oh, yes. They do sometimes."

"Daddy?"

"Yes,"

"Where did Uncle George go?"

"He'll turn up all right."

"Is dying hard, Daddy?"

"No, I think it's pretty easy, Nick. It all depends."

[Hemingway, *In Our Time*, 1925]

2 "I suppose my thoughts are nothing to be proud of," said Eleanor Sullivan.

"Then they are different from the rest of you, I am sure, dear."

"I always mean what I say, Fulbert." ...

"If you reveal the thoughts, I will give them my attention," he said, leaning back and folding his arms with this purpose.

"It is the old grievance of spending my best years in your parents' home."

"It would be worse not to spend them in a home of any kind."

"You must turn everything into a joke of course."

[I. Compton-Burnett, *Parents and Children*, 1941]

3 "I know its meaning now," he muttered, "and the restless nights, the dreams, and why I have quailed of late. All pointed to this. Oh! if men by selling their own souls could ride rampant for a term, for how short a term would I barter mine tonight!"

The sound of a deep bell came along the wind. One.

"Lie on!" cried the usurer, "with your iron tongue! Ring merrily for births that make expectants writhe, and for marriages that are made in hell, and toll ruefully for the dead whose shoes are worn already! Call men to prayers who are godly because not found out, and ring chimes for the coming in of every year that brings this cursed world nearer to its end. No bell or book for me! Throw me on a dunghill, and let me rot there, to infect the air!"   [Dickens, *Nicholas Nickleby*, 1839]

4 "Now, my own, own love," she whispered, "you are mine, and only mine; for she has forgot 'ee at last, although for her you died! But I – whenever I get up I'll think of 'ee, and whenever I lie down I'll think of 'ee again. Whenever I plant the young larches I'll think that none can plant as you planted; and whenever I split a gad, and whenever I turn the cider wring, I'll say none could do it like you. If ever I forget your name let me forget home and heaven! ... But no, no, my love, I never can forget 'ee; for you was a good man, and did good things!"

[Hardy, *The Woodlanders*, 1887]

5 "Aw'd rayther he'd goan hisseln fur t' doctor! Aw sud uh taen tent uh
t'maister better nur him – un he warn't deead when Aw left, nowt uh
t'soart!"   [E. Brontë, *Wuthering Heights*, 1847]

The first three of these extracts stand at various points on a continuum
which ranges from the extreme of realism to that of convention. Hemingway conveys a sense of deeply-felt issues through a dialogue remarkable
for its economy and simplicity: whereas Dickens attempts to devise a
language proportionate to the intensity of the imagined situation,
Hemingway works by means of a deliberate contrast between calculatedly
trite expressions, unafraid of cliché, and the largeness of the ideas and emotions implied. His structure is the simplest one available to the writer of
dialogue, that of the catechism or cross-examination; and the father's replies to the boy's simple but searching questions combine complete
seriousness with colloquial understatement ('"He couldn't stand things, I
guess"', where that deliberately awkward *things* is a kind of guarantee of
integrity; *cf* the deprecatory epithet in '"I think it's *pretty* easy"'). The
longest sentence in the passage quoted contains seven words; the average
sentence-length is under four words; and no word occurs which might
not plausibly be found in the spontaneous speech of even a child. *This*, we
may be tempted to observe, is surely an accurate transcript from life itself –
the novelist as tape-recorder. And yet the dialogue has a directness, a sureness and sense of purpose, which are very different from the hesitations,
false starts, repetitions, corrections and contradictions and changes of
direction of normal speech. It represents, that is to say, an *idealization* of
real speech, with a ruthless paring away of superfluities, rather than a
wholehearted attempt at faithfully reproducing it. And, as in life, the
dialogue makes no pretence of being self-sufficient or fully self-explanatory, but derives much of its resonance from a knowledge of the full
context of the story in which it appears. Thus, the simple exchange

"Where did Uncle George go?"
"He'll turn up all right."

though trite enough in itself, can be seen as an ironic comment on character by the reader who is already acquainted with Uncle George's behaviour, and the casual *all right* conveys a tone of indulgence if not con-
tempt.

If Hemingway seeks to offer us at any rate the appearance of the natural
grain of the wood, Ivy Compton-Burnett in (2) invites us to admire the
results of some assiduous French-polishing. Even granting the obvious
differences between the speakers in the two passages, it is clear that a dif-

ferent kind of convention is at work. Whilst it is not incredible that any individual speech might be uttered in actuality, the cumulative effect of these exchanges has a most unlifelike elegance and pointedness, resembling that created by an anthology of the 'wit and wisdom' of a brilliant conversationalist, a Sydney Smith or Oscar Wilde. One misses the element of occasional diffuseness, the hit-or-miss quality of real-life conversation which aspires to be witty. What differentiates it from Hemingway's dialogue is the degree of verbal self-awareness on the part of the speakers, especially Fulbert: instead of father and child talking about the mysteries of life and death in the only language they have in common, we are presented with two highly articulate persons, at least one of whom takes an obvious pleasure in scoring points in a verbal tennis-match. Fulbert's ripostes give a formal quality to the dialogue which makes the first six speeches quoted, for instance, fall as neatly into 'couplets' as a passage of Pope's verse, and with something of the same effect. Here the relationship between statement and response is a more subtle one than that of the simple question-and-answer pattern found in (1). The first speaker makes a series of statements, particular verbal elements in which (eg, *thoughts*, *home*) are taken up by her interlocutor. This consciousness of words as well as meanings also affects the reader's reaction to dialogue of this kind, which can be read for the aesthetic pleasure it provides – as an end in itself, that is (though it is not merely that), rather than as deriving its full meaning only from a wider context. The average sentence-length is eleven words – about three times that of Hemingway – the sentences being structurally much closer to those of written prose.

The relationship to a variety of written English is even closer in (3), where indeed it would be hard to claim that any significant relationship to real speech is to be traced. Dickens's source for the dramatic monologue of Ralph Nickleby is, plainly enough, to be found less in his observation of the language of men than in certain literary and theatrical prototypes. The 'iron tongue' of the conveniently-sounding bell (perhaps an echo of the final scene of Marlowe's *Dr Faustus*?), the anaphoric series of imperatives (*Lie, Ring, toll, Call*, etc), the metrical element in '"Ring merrily for births that make expectants writhe"' – such devices belong to a common stock of literary, and especially dramatic and poetic, language. Such an observation should be taken, however, as descriptive rather than critical: the fact that vocabulary, structures and rhythms derive from an established idiom limits the possibilities of originality, and interferes with the sense of probability, but is not in itself necessarily a fault, provided one is prepared to admit that the convention of such dialogue in fiction, like that of the blank-verse soliloquy to which it is obviously related, belongs to a frankly non-realistic genre. Here, however, it is possible to say, with more confidence than in respect of the previous extract, that no man has under any circumstances ever spoken quite as Dickens's villain does here (unless, of course, he was imitating, seriously or facetiously, the rhetorical tradition represented by Ralph Nickleby).

In (4), Marty South's soliloquy in the final paragraph of *The Wood-landers* is more readily acceptable as a plausible utterance. The language is heightened by emotion but still contains reminders of the speaker's humble background in the non-standard forms ('*ee, you was*) and in the precise but entirely natural terms in which she refers to rural activities. Such reminders of regional, social and occupational background are used, however, with notable discretion: they are occasional signals rather than part of a consistent effort to reproduce the features of non-standard speech in detail. For Hardy, the virtues of clarity and intelligibility are paramount. The use of parallelism, which might be objected to as some-what self-consciously literary, may be defended as the natural modification of Marty's native woodnotes, under the stress of powerful feelings, by her unconscious recollections of Biblical idiom – probably the only literary influence to which such a girl, in such a time and place, would have been subjected. The literary influence is thus a much more acceptable one than those detected in Ralph Nickleby's speech. However, the skilfully-contrived movement towards a climax betrays a conscious artistic purpose, which not even the apparent artlessness of the final phrases – the deliberate awkwardness of 'good things', like the calculatedly rough-hewn quality of the diction in much of Hardy's poetry, seems intended to reassure the reader as to the fundamental sincerity of the work – is entirely successful in concealing. Closer analysis shows that the whole of the passage quoted is constructed on a principle of repetition and balance which becomes pro-gressively more complex: the simple reiterations in the opening sentence (*own, own; mine . . . mine; she . . . her*) are followed by the more complex reiteration of a larger unit (main clause + subordinate clause) in the second sentence, and of a still larger one, with some modification in the repetition to prevent its becoming merely mechanical, in the third sentence. The climactic fourth sentence is shorter but contains both the repeated *forget*, balancing its two clauses, and the alliterative *home and heaven*. To refer to Marty's speech as 'simple', therefore, while legitimately describing its literary effect, is to give an inaccurate account of the verbal means used to obtain that effect. Both arrangement and selectivity, the indispensable techniques of the dialogue-writer, are at work in this passage.

In contrast to Marty South, Emily Brontë's Yorkshire servant Joseph is given a form of speech which embodies a much more thorough and detailed attempt at conveying a regional flavour – in this case, a West Riding dialect. The frequency of dialectal terms, and of non-standard spellings to indicate pronunciation, may well be regarded as obstacles to comprehension, for Emily Brontë is not afraid to present the reader with problems which Hardy more considerately, or more timidly, spares him. (Indeed, as will later be shown, the text of *Wuthering Heights* in general use today offers only a proportion of the linguistic difficulties originally forming part of the author's purpose.) Yet the attempt, though more ambitious than Hardy's, is necessarily still selective and partial – a calculated gesture towards authenticity rather than (what no work of fiction can ever offer) a completely accurate and consistent transcript of the living dialect. In other words, in speaking of dialogue, 'realism' is a relative term, even the more extreme examples being found on examination to retain to some degree their conventional elements.

Many questions are raised even by brief samples of dialogue such as those quoted. What is the effect, in terms of the reader's response during the act of reading, of written dialogue, whether or not accompanied by such aids and directions as variant spellings and sensitively orchestrated punctuation devices? and in what sense can such an experience be said to approximate to the actual hearing of speech? With what consistency are these orthographic and other systems used, and what substitutes for them may be found? What influence does non-standard speech of various kinds have upon our assessment of character in fiction – would Joseph's speech, for instance, however successful as it stands, be thinkable for a major character or a tragic or pathetic role? Or has it perhaps been more thinkable as such in some periods than in others – what, that is to say, have been the main historical changes in attitude towards varieties of dialogue? And, while all fictional speech is to some extent non-realistic, what of the category represented by the quotation from Dickens, where even the pretence of realism is rejected: what effect does such dialogue have upon the status of the characters concerned, and, more generally, upon our notions of the ultimate intention of the novel in which it appears? Some of these questions, it is plain, relate not only to the internal nature of dialogue but to its place in a novel in relation to other elements. For no novelist can avoid continually exercising a choice between different modes of presentation: at any point – in the introduction of a character, for instance, or the rendering of a dramatic episode, or the presentation of necessary information – he must choose between dialogue and narrative or descriptive prose, or a combination of these in proportions which must be settled. If he decides to make use of dialogue, a further selection has to be made among the various ways of presenting speech. We can ask, therefore, of any novel, whether speech habitually carries the main burden of fictional business or whether this duty is partly or largely performed by other means; and we can also ask the more specifically stylistic question, What linguistic differences exist between dialogue and non-dialogue writing? The chapters which follow raise these questions again, both in general terms and in relation to specific texts.

Notes

1 M. Schorer, 'Technique as Discovery', *Hudson Review*, 1, 1948, 68.
2 W. Allen, *The English Novel*, Harmondsworth, 1958, 14.
3 In an essay titled 'The Art of Fiction' published in 1884, and reprinted in *Henry James: Selected Literary Criticism*, ed M. Schapira, 1963, 58. James's view may be compared with that of a more recent writer, I. A. Gordon: 'Viewed (so to speak) anatomically, a novel consists of four prose "systems": dialogue, narrative, description, and commentary. In many twentieth-century novels, the systems overlap and run together ... but this is a comparatively late development in the novel' (*The Movement of English Prose*, 1966, 162). The last part of Gordon's comment seems highly arguable.
4 I. A. Gordon, *op cit*, 162; D. Lodge, *Language of Fiction*, 1966, 47; S. Ullmann, *Style in the French Novel*, 1957, 257 (the reference is to Sartre's *La Mort dans l'Ame*).
5 Quoted in *A Linguistics Reader*, ed G. Wilson, New York, 1967, 249.
6 R. Quirk, *The English Language and Images of Matter*, 1972, Chs 10 and 12. D. Crystal and D. Davy, *Investigating English Style*, 1969, Ch 4.
7 *Athenaeum*, 30 November 1878; quoted by E. Brennecke, *Life and Art by Thomas Hardy*, New York, 1925, 114–15.
8 Quoted by J. C. Gerber, 'Point of View in Mark Twain', in *Style in Prose Fiction*, ed H. C. Martin, New York, 1959, 163.
9 R. L. Stevenson, *Letters*, ed S. Colvin, 1906, I, 341.
10 P. Young, in *Seven Modern American Novelists*, ed W. Van O'Connor, 1965, 181.
11 J. Sutherland, Introduction to *The Oxford Book of English Talk*, 1953, ix.

Further references

D. Abercrombie, 'Conversation and Spoken Prose', in *Studies in Phonetics and Linguistics*, 1965, 1–9.
E. Bentley, *The Life of the Drama*, 1965.
M. Evans, 'Elizabethan Spoken English', *Cambridge Journal*, 4, 1951, 401–14.
A. McIntosh and M. Halliday, *Patterns of Language*, 1966.
R. Quirk, *The Use of English*, 1968.

M. Riffaterre, 'Criteria for Style Analysis', *Word*, 15, 1959, 154–74.

A. H. Smith and R. Quirk, 'Some Problems of Verbal Communication', *Transactions of the Yorkshire Dialect Society*, 9, 1955, 10–20.

J. Spencer (ed), *Linguistics and Style*, 1964.

P. Strevens, 'Varieties of English', in *Papers in Language and Language Teaching*, 1965, 74–86 (and *cf* G. L. Brook, 'Varieties of English', *Bulletin of the John Rylands Library, Manchester*, 51, 1969, 271–91).

G. H. Vallins, *The Best English*, 1960, Ch 5 ('Speech in Literature').

R. Wellek and A. Warren, *Theory of Literature*, 1966, Ch 16.

H. C. Wyld, *A History of Modern Colloquial English*, 1936.

Chapter 2

Methods of speech-presentation

Before examining more extensively the varieties and functions assumed by speech in fiction, the forms in which it can be presented must detain us briefly. Every schoolboy knows that there are two ways of setting down speech: in the direct and the indirect (or reported) forms; but anyone who reads the dialogue in novels at all carefully soon becomes aware that these simple and clearly-defined categories, ultimately inherited from the study of the classical languages, completely fail to accommodate many passages to be found in the work of writers from the eighteenth century onwards. The truth is that we lack both an adequate framework of definition and an adequate terminology by means of which the practice of English writers may be described and analysed. (As in many areas of stylistics, writers in the Romance languages have been better served than English authors; and such attention as has been paid to writing in English has come largely from continental scholars.) The present chapter must concern itself, therefore, both with the familiar categories and with others lying between or outside them.

At every point at which a novelist wishes to convey an impression of the use of speech, he is forced to make a conscious or unconscious choice between the various forms available. (Not every form, of course, has been equally at the disposal of every generation.) If we assume for the moment a hypothetical notion of the 'actual words spoken' in the fictional world of his creation, his choice will determine how close to, or how remote from, those 'actual words spoken' his presentation of speech will be. He may decide to adopt the role of the dramatist and, by the use of direct speech, to allow his characters to 'speak for themselves'. There is usually no problem in recognizing direct speech, consisting as it does of the actual words the reader is to suppose to have been uttered by a character in dialogue, monologue or soliloquy, and normally accompanied by the appropriate graphological indications (though these, as examples from the *Authorized Version* to Joyce's *Ulysses* show, are by no means indispensable).

The various indications of direct speech have been described as 'invitations to an auditory experience',[1] but this description needs modification to suggest that what is in question is, rather, the provision of hints towards an imaginative reconstruction of speech by the reader on the basis of his empirical knowledge of speech and his familiarity with the conventions of written dialogue. The psycholinguistic question of what *happens* when various readers (silently) read a passage of dialogue – of how the experience differs, on the one hand, from hearing speech and, on the other, from reading passages of non-dialogue prose – is a fascinating and complex one. Probably there is considerable variation between individuals, related to (among other things) reading speed and accuracy of aural memory, as well as an important degree of difference according to the writer's mode of presentation.

In its purest form a passage may consist so largely of direct speech, so little diluted with other elements, as to resemble an extract from a play. (The quotations from Hemingway and Compton-Burnett in the last chapter belong to this category.) This is perhaps the point to recall, even at the expense of a brief digression, that the English novel drew a considerable portion of its sustenance in the earlier phases of its development from the drama. Defoe, in *Roxana, Colonel Jack*, and other novels, habitually sets out his dialogue in dramatic form; Richardson was very fond of what he described as 'the rational diversion of a good play' and, according to a recent critic, 'got a diversity of techniques and materials from his knowledge of plays';[2] Fielding, like Dickens and Henry James later, wrote for the stage as well as the novel-reader, and his experience as a comic dramatist can be traced in the deft handling of situation and dialogue in many scenes of *Tom Jones*. The tradition is a continuous one: in our own time, Graham Greene, Angus Wilson, William Golding and Muriel Spark among others have written for stage, film or radio. Moreover, the novel in the course of its history usurped some of the social functions of the theatre, the rise of the former being accompanied by the decline of the latter. The greatest period of the English novel, the Victorian age, is also that in which the native drama sank almost into insignificance. In the eighteenth-century novel, when the art of fiction is still in the process of discovering its own techniques and is therefore apt to lean most heavily on established genres, the reader often has the sense of the novelist providing equivalents for theatrical elements which must necessarily, in the novel medium, be rendered verbally. Thus passages of description replace the direct visual impact of scenery, costumes, and the movements of the actors, and narrative is a natural development from stage-directions.[3]

It is in dialogue, of course, that the two genres approximate most closely to each other, and where the art of the dramatist could be transferred with a minimum of adaptation to the novel. Many scenes in Richardson and Fielding suggest that they were conceived in terms of the stage. However, the advantages of the novel-medium in being able to present, in constantly varying proportions, both dialogue and as much or as little complementary and supplementary description, information or comment as the author may desire, are too real to be disregarded. Direct speech is generally accompanied, therefore, by some or all of the following:

[1] attributions to speakers, often necessary to avoid confusion or tedious calculation on the reader's part, and an obvious example of a substitution for an element provided in the theatre by the physical presence of the actors. It may be noted that many writers seek to relieve the monotony of constant 'he-saids' by resorting to elegant variation, though the variations, when not simply a novelistic habit, are in themselves expressive. The opening chapter of *David Copperfield* has *returned* eight times, *asked* and *cried* five times each, *exclaimed, faltered* and *resumed* twice each, and *repeated, replied, sobbed, mused* and *ejaculating* once each, as well as *said* thirty-seven times; only two very short sentences are not explicitly attributed to a speaker.

[2] 'stage-directions' as to facial expression, movement, gesture, etc – the expressive accompaniments of speech. The theatrical element in the eighteenth-century novel has already been referred to, and in Fielding such 'stage-directions' are often introduced into a passage of speech as they might be into a dramatic script: thus Lady Booby in *Joseph Andrews* recalls her dead husband, saying that

> "... the dear man who is gone" (*here she began to sob*), "was he alive again" (*then she produced tears*), "could not upbraid me with any one act of tenderness or passion."

Naturally enough, the practice of different novelists in this respect varies widely, in accordance with the extent to which their dialogue is conceived in dramatic and visual terms. Jane Austen, for example, who is more concerned with the moral implications of a scene than with rendering its circumstantiality, uses them sparingly, whereas they are abundant in Dickens, as the often-noted theatrical element in his work would lead one to expect. Related to them are

[3] references to or indications of paralinguistic qualities such as stress,

pitch, intonation, volume, vocal quality, either within the dialogue itself
(by, for instance, such devices as capitalization, italicization and hyphenation) or in the accompanying comments ('he muttered', 'she shrieked',
etc). To draw attention to them by direct comment is to throw the major
burden of reconstructing a particular variety of speech upon the reader, for
an indication such as 'he lisped' will serve little purpose in the dialogue
unless the reader is prepared to take it into account in his inner experience
of reading it, just as he is required to reproduce the appropriate behaviour
from his own observation and memory if he is reading the passage aloud.
By well-established convention, a single indication of this kind permits the
dialogue itself to be given 'straight', that is, without further formal indications of eccentricity. The method has the obvious advantage of being less
troublesome for both author and reader: the lispings of Mr Sleary in
Hard Times not only gave Dickens a good deal of trouble (as his manuscript makes plain) but can quickly prove irksome and tedious in the
reading, since they are permitted to interfere with normal orthography to
the extent of slowing down the reader considerably. On the other hand,
they do virtually compel the reader to 'listen' to Mr Sleary, even if he is
reading silently. Another advantage of the once-and-for-all indication
outside the dialogue itself is that it can enable the writer to suggest
features of speech which the written language is not equipped to represent
adequately – an inflection or tone that may be meaningful but quite beyond the power of the printer's symbols to convey. How, for example,
could such favourite formulae attached to dialogue as 'he chuckled' or
'she hinted darkly' be otherwise rendered? The major disadvantage of the
method lies in the surrender of the comic or dramatic possibilities of
eccentric dialogue, and in the risk that the rapid or careless reader may
completely overlook the characteristic in question. Emily Brontë's per-
sistence in rendering the Yorkshire dialect of Joseph, already illustrated,
makes a contribution to the grotesque and uncouth impression created by
this character in *Wuthering Heights* that could scarcely have been achieved
by a simple reference to his broad local dialect. (At the same time, one
might well enquire what would be the effect of Joseph's speech on, say,
an Australian or West African reader totally unfamiliar with West
Riding speech, and whether the internal representation of his pronunciation achieves something that could not otherwise have been obtained.) The
two different methods may be illustrated by contrasting two passages by
Dickens. When Mr Pecksniff is intoxicated (*Martin Chuzzlewit*, Ch 9), we
are told that he speaks 'with imperfect articulation', and there are subsequent reminders of his condition in references to his 'thick and husky

voice' and his 'stuttering', but the dialogue itself bears no orthographic or other evidence of this state. David Copperfield's inebriation, on the other hand, is manifested both within and outside the dialogue: '"Agnes!" I said thickly, "Lorblessmer! Agnes!"' (*David Copperfield*, Ch 24). There can be little doubt which example arrests the reader's attention more readily by its linguistic vitality.

[4] finally, many novelists find the temptation to interpolate comment or moralizing into dialogue passages quite irresistible. Perhaps none goes further in this respect than Sterne in *Tristram Shandy*: in the famous scene in which Bobby's death is reported to the servants by Corporal Trim (Bk V, Ch 7), the dialogue is almost submerged by the tide of commentary and analysis.

The use of direct speech within a given episode may be conveniently illustrated from the trial scene in the thirty-fourth chapter of *The Pickwick Papers* (with special attention to the passage from 'The judge had no sooner taken his seat . . .' to '. . . out of court'). Its dramatic quality, in its use of speech to reveal character as well as further the action, is evident, and it later became one of Dickens's most successful public readings. Well over half the passage in question consists of direct speech, and there is a generous use of what have been loosely referred to as 'stage-directions': 'with interesting agitation', 'with a cunning look', etc. At the same time one notes several useful devices which are not at the dramatist's disposal. A phrase such as 'after a few unimportant questions' enables the novelist to dispense with a potentially low-pressure stretch of dialogue in a way that would be difficult to achieve on the stage. Similarly, we are told that 'Mrs Cluppins repeated the conversation with which our readers are already acquainted', and 'our readers' are accordingly not subjected to the tedium of repetition. Again, the browbeating of Mr Winkle is presented with notable economy by the partial use of indirect speech, which also provides stylistic variety. Although the scene contains, therefore, a high proportion of direct speech – and it is significant that when Dickens came to prepare his reading version very few changes were necessary to turn the novel-text into a dramatic script – the novelist has taken advantage of the possibilities of manipulating the tempo of his episode and the angle of its presentation in a manner that belongs distinctively to the written medium.

Three common conventions in the use of direct speech should be briefly referred to. One is the custom of reproducing dialogue, even in a first-person narrative, without any reservations as to its accuracy or completeness: thus, conversations which are supposed to have taken place many years earlier are often given intact in all their details. This species of total recall on the narrator's part is a natural, and easily-accepted, convention of the medium. A more technical convention relates to the expectations aroused by the use of quotation marks and other graphological and typo-graphical indications that 'actual speech' is being offered. In earlier periods, and certainly until the beginning of the nineteenth century, quotation marks were used in certain contexts where they would not nowadays be employed. In Fielding, for example, we find the following:

> Meeting the landlady, he accosted her with great civility, and asked "What he could have for dinner?"   [*Tom Jones*, VIII, 4]

The usage is found as late as Jane Austen, but by the time of Dickens the quotation marks have disappeared:

> He checks his horse and asks a workman does he know the name of Rouncewell thereabouts?   [*Bleak House*, Ch 63]

Such examples, though not identical in grammatical structure, show a common movement towards the integration of direct speech with narra-tive style – a tendency to which we must shortly turn. There remains to be noted a third convention, much favoured by Jane Austen, whereby the novelist is permitted to conflate into a single speech what must probably be supposed to have been uttered as several separate speeches. The gain in speed and concentration of effect is considerable. Consider, for example, Mr Woodhouse's characteristic expressions of anxiety in the third chapter of *Emma*:

> "Mrs Bates, let me propose your venturing on one of these eggs. An egg boiled very soft is not unwholesome. Serle understands boiling an egg better than anybody . . . Miss Bates, let Emma help you to a *little* bit of tart – a *very* little bit. Ours are all apple-tarts. You need not be afraid of unwholesome preserves here. I do not advise the custard. Mrs Goddard, what say you to *half* a glass of wine? A *small* half glass, put into a tumbler of water? . . ."

Jane Austen has caught the timidity of Mr Woodhouse in the face of ex-perience, even experience taking the mild form of an apple-tart, and has found linguistic equivalents for it in his speech, with its repeated negatives and diminutives. It seems unlikely, however, that this would have been delivered as an uninterrupted monologue, since Woodhouse addresses three ladies in turn, of whom Miss Bates at least would hardly have re-mained silent; and the passage quoted might well have been presented as three separate speeches with appropriate responses interspersed. More important than these unreported replies, however, is the cumulative effect of the old gentleman's frettings, and his conversation is presented as monologue in the interests of clarity of character-portrayal. A more glaring example, which invites comparison with the final speech of Marlowe's *Dr Faustus*, occurs in *Northanger Abbey*. Anxiously awaiting her friends, and hearing the clock strike twelve, Catherine Morland declares:

> "I do not quite despair yet. I shall not give it up till a quarter after twelve. This is just the time of day for it to clear up, and I do think it looks a little lighter. There, it is twenty minutes after twelve, and now I *shall* give it up entirely . . ."

Unblushingly, the novelist permits twenty minutes to elapse during the uttering of less than forty words. Quite clearly, the force of the quotation marks in this example is different from that in most direct speech: a protracted conversation, or at least a one-sided series of remarks, has been telescoped into a single speech in the interests of narrative economy. By such means can the tendency to diffuseness inherent in the use of direct speech be circumvented. A different kind of convention operates in the vulgar Mrs Elton's raptures over the strawberry-picking (*Emma*, Ch 42):

> "The best fruit in England – every body's favourite – always wholesome. These the finest beds and finest sorts. – Delightful to gather for one's self – the only way of really enjoying them . . ."

– and so on, at considerable length. The gist of many long and tedious speeches is conveyed through a drastically abridged monologue, involving the sacrifice of most of the main verbs – the abridgement itself implying an ironic comment on the speaker's wearisome volubility. As with Miss Bates in the same novel, we have the impression of tedium without suffering its effects. Again, although we cannot suppose that Mrs Elton would continue at such length without even the encouragement of a sympathetic murmur, all other participants in the conversation have been eliminated, so that what we encounter is not so much a transcript of a supposed dialogue as a heavily edited version of it. With this last example, indeed, we begin to move away from direct speech proper in the direction of the freer forms.

Direct speech, therefore, is not a single method but can range from the undoctored to the stylized, though its distinctive virtue lies in its capacity for allowing a character to 'speak', in an individual voice, directly to the reader without the appearance of authorial intervention. Its advantages are its immediacy and the stylistic variety attainable in dialogue which can offer lexical and syntactical contrasts to the other portions of a novel; its limitations are a tendency towards diffuseness and a consequent thinness of effect, and the need for frequent 'gear-shifting' – not always easily accomplished – in the change from non-dialogue to dialogue elements and back again. Indirect speech can offer a gain in pace and economy by way of compensation for the loss of immediacy; it also combines more readily with narrative style, making possible a free movement from one to the other. But even less than the direct variety is indirect speech a single, unvarying form. Although it traditionally employs (in parliamentary reporting, for example) a neutral style, it need not in the novel necessarily involve a total renunciation of the attempt to represent individual varieties of speech. It can assume some of the normal features of the indirect form whilst retaining others which belong to the direct form. Thus we need to be aware of 'degrees of indirectness', some sense of which may be appreciated by considering the differences displayed by a handful of brief quotations:

1 Lydia was bid by her two eldest sisters to hold her tongue ... Turning to Mr Bennet, he (Mr Collins) offered himself as his antagonist at backgammon.   [Austen, *Pride and Prejudice*, Ch 14]

2 Mrs Bickerton assured her, that the acceptance of any reckoning was entirely out of the question ...   [Scott, *The Heart of Midlothian*, Ch 28]

3 The doctor accused Mr Allworthy of too great lenity, repeated his accusations against his brother, and declared that he should never more be brought either to see, or to own him for his relation.
                                   [Fielding, *Tom Jones*, I, Ch 12]

4 Mr Sapsea expressed his opinion that the case had a dark look; in short (and here his eyes rested full on Neville's countenance), an un-English complexion.   [Dickens, *Edwin Drood*, Ch 15]

5 Mrs O'Dowd [described] how it had been presented to her by her fawther, as she stipt into the car'ge after her mar'ge.
                                   [Thackeray, *Vanity Fair*, Ch 28]

Of all these extracts, each of which implies the use of speech by a named character, we may ask the same question: To what extent may the 'original words spoken' be reconstructed from the indirect form? The answers given will be very different, however. The examples from Austen belong to narrative style, though there is a clear indication that speech has taken place. The reader has no means of reconstructing the specific stylistic

features of the 'original' utterances; and though it is quite conceivable
that the pompous Mr Collins should have proposed a game by offering
himself as an 'antagonist', and equally likely that one or both of Lydia's
sisters used the unladylike expression 'hold your tongue', these expressions may equally possibly belong only to the narrative style and in no way
imply a verbal echo of the speeches that lie behind it. The reader is simply
not in a position to know. What saves the question from being purely
pedantic is the not unimportant matter of how far a given style enables the
reader to 'hear' a distinctive speaking voice which, by its particular qualities, contributes to dramatic situation and character-development. What
we have here is not indirect speech in the ordinary sense, but what might
(1) be termed 'submerged speech': the supposed dialogue has become absorbed by the narrative, with consequent likely changes of lexis as well as a
grammatical form different from that of indirect speech (since it lacks the
subordinate clause or clauses dependent on a verb of saying). It thus differs
from the example in (2), which belongs to the category of ordinary or
traditional indirect speech: the main clause identifies the speaker and includes the verb of saying, whilst the subordinate clause conveys the substance of the speech and involves a tense-shift (in this case, from present to
past). But this indirect version bears little stylistic evidence of the colloquial origin of the speech reported, since the landlady's remark has become
subdued to the formal style of Scott's narrative. This we may regard as indirect speech proper, in which a neutral reporting style irons out the possible eccentricities of the individual 'original' speeches.

The next example combines the two forms already identified. The first
half of Fielding's sentence (to 'brother') indicates summarily the content of
what was obviously a speech of some length, but the second half moves
from editorial summary to indirect speech as defined above. A new element is found in the sentence from *Edwin Drood*, which seems to bear the
outward tokens of indirect speech but is significantly different from the
earlier example from Scott. In its subordinate clause it forsakes a neutral
reporting style and, for the sake of the wordplay, reproduces the phrases
'a dark look' and 'an un-English complexion' intact from the direct
speech implied. In this case, therefore, the use of indirect speech does not
prevent the reader from 'hearing' Mr Sapsea in his individuality and does
not entail an inevitable sacrifice of immediacy and vividness. Finally, the
quotation from Thackeray shows that features of phonology as well as of
lexis and syntax are within its scope: even the orthography of the indirect
version is susceptible to 'colouring' by the Anglo-Irish pronunciation of
Mrs O'Dowd.

In the light of examples such as these, the simple and attractive antithesis that 'Direct speech is natural speech. Indirect speech is artificial speech'[4] is hardly acceptable in relation to the novel. Such an antithesis only obscures the considerable common element which exists *between* the two kinds, as well as the varieties distinguishable *within* each kind. In the whole question of forms of speech-presentation, indeed, what is encountered is not so much a set of rigid categories, each with its own exclusive and unmistakable identifying features, as a merging of one form with another and with narrative style. Nor, though the question has traditionally been treated as a grammatical one, can the placing of a particular instance always be made solely on the basis of grammatical features. As suggested above, the need exists to distinguish further between at least two kinds of indirect speech: that which enables the reader to deduce some of the structural and lexical features of the original, and that in which these features have become absorbed by the style deemed appropriate for the reported version. For the purposes of illustration, and to show that there are further 'degrees of indirectness' which need to be distinguished within each of these two kinds, the simple exercise may be performed of recasting a single short speech in several different ways. In Chapter 25 of Dickens's *Martin Chuzzlewit* we find the following example of direct speech:

"There are some happy creeturs," Mrs Gamp observed, "as time runs back'ards with, and you are one, Mrs Mould . . ."

This possesses certain features which may be regarded as contributing to the peculiar vitality and variety of direct speech: non-standard grammar to suggest a particular social dialect, variant spellings to suggest distinctive qualities of pronunciation, the use of a form of address. We may ask to what extent these may be preserved in the various forms of indirect speech. To begin at the point remotest from the original: the sentence might have been presented as what has been termed 'submerged speech', in some such form as

1 Mrs Gamp complimented Mrs Mould on her youthful appearance.

This indicates that speech has taken place but retains none of the idiosyncrasies of the original: lexically, it is formal and literary; grammatically, it is beyond reproach; and there is no implication of non-standard pronunciation. Or it might have appeared as indirect speech in any one of a number of ways. For example:

2 Mrs Gamp observed that some fortunate people, of whom Mrs Mould was one, seemed to be unaffected by time.

3 Mrs Gamp observed that there were some happy creatures that time ran backwards with, and that Mrs Mould was one of them.

4 Mrs Gamp observed that there were some happy creeturs as time ran back'ards with, and that Mrs Mould was one of them.

All of these follow the normal structural conventions of indirect speech (verb of saying + that (may be omitted) + subordinate clause with verb in past tense and pronouns in third person); but they stand at varying distances from the direct speech on which they are based. (2) is farthest from it, and amounts to a virtual paraphrase: syntax apart, it has much in common with (1). (4), on the other hand, preserves many features of the original, including its orthographic variants, and may be conveniently referred to as 'coloured' or 'modified' indirect speech. (3) falls between these two extremes, and may perhaps reasonably be termed 'parallel indirect speech', on account of its lexical faithfulness to the original. There are, of course, many other possible variations, but only two call for special mention:

5 There were some happy creatures that time ran backwards with, and Mrs Mould was one of them.

6 Mrs Gamp observed that there were some happy creatures that time ran backwards with, 'and you are one, Mrs Mould'.

In (5) the use of *free* indirect speech is characterized by the absence of indication of speaker. (A further variation would be to modify this version by reproducing the original spelling of *creeturs* and *back'ards*.) In (6) we have an example of what has been termed 'slipping' from indirect into direct speech[5] – the character's voice interrupting the narrator's, as it were; again a further variation is possible by the omission of the quotation marks.

The main features of the various forms so far identified may be summarized as shown in the table on page 35.

Free indirect speech, briefly referred to above, now calls for further discussion. Though identified and discussed by linguists only in this century, free indirect speech (also known as *style indirect libre* and *erlebte Rede*) is used by a number of nineteenth-century authors from Jane Austen onwards.[6] An even earlier example occurs in a novel Jane Austen knew well, Fanny Burney's *Evelina* (1778):

> . . . Lord Orville saw and approached me.
> He begged to know if I was not well?
> He then . . . asked if he had been so unhappy as to offend me?

Type of speech	Grammatical features		Lexical features	
	1	2	1	2
	introductory verb of saying (usually that)	subordinate clause in past tense	neutral or idiosyncratic[a]	possible indication of phonological qualities
A: Direct	no	no	idiosyncratic	yes
B: 'Submerged'	yes	no	neutral	no
C: Indirect	yes	yes	neutral	no[b]
D: 'Parallel' indirect	yes	yes	idiosyncratic	no
E: 'Coloured' indirect	yes	yes	idiosyncratic	yes
F: Free indirect	no	no	idiosyncratic	no
G: Free direct[c]	no	no	idiosyncratic	yes

H: 'Slipping' from indirect into direct speech involves a mid-sentence change from C to A.

[a] 'Neutral': lexically undifferentiated with regard to the individual speaker. 'Idiosyncratic': reflecting the qualities (often grammatical as well as lexical) of the 'original' speech.

[b] Or, exceptionally, 'yes', as in the example from *Vanity Fair*.

[c] Graphological indications of direct speech are also omitted; this form seems relatively rare in English. (See L. C. Harmer, *The French Language Today*, 1954, 300–301)

> "No, indeed!" cried I; and . . . I desired to know if he had seen the young lady who had been conversing with me?
>
> *No; – but would I honour him with my commands to see her?*
>
> "O, by no means!"
>
> *Was there any other person with whom I wished to speak? . . .*
>
> [*Evelina*, Letter XI; my italics]

In this short passage we find an interesting combination of direct speech (reserved for the heroine-narrator), indirect speech, and free indirect speech (italicized) for Lord Orville's later remarks. The author's purpose seems to be to retain her heroine as the centre of attention by permitting Evelina's narrating 'voice' to continue without interruption: Orville is distanced since both the indirect and the free indirect forms serve a common aim of mediating his remarks through Evelina, but the switch from indirect to free indirect marks a slight but perceptible rise in dramatic urgency.

Jane Austen's usage goes well beyond anything to be found in Fanny Burney, and may be briefly illustrated from *Persuasion* (1818) – a novel in which she can be seen to have moved towards a remarkably flexible conception of speech-presentation.[7] Both examples occur in the same passage in Chapter 20:

> . . . she found herself accosted by Captain Wentworth, in a reserved yet hurried sort of farewell. "He must wish her good night. He was going – he should get home as fast as he could."

> . . . But alas! there were very different thoughts to succeed. How was such jealousy to be quieted? How was the truth to reach him? How, in all the peculiar disadvantages of their respective situations, would he ever learn her real sentiments?

The first of these follows eighteenth-century practice in enclosing the substance of Wentworth's speech in quotation marks, though it is clearly not his 'actual words' that we are given. The use of free indirect speech here, in place of the more usual direct form, has the effect of merging dialogue with narrative and retaining the consistent viewpoint of the heroine, whose emotional state remains the centre of attention. Part of the smoothness of the transition from narrative to speech is owed to the fact that the first- and second-person pronouns of direct speech can, in free indirect speech, appear as the third-person pronouns normal in narrative. At the same time, the brief, urgent statements have the dramatic impact of direct speech, the syntax suggesting dialogue rather than formal narrative prose. In the second example, thoughts rather than speech are in question: Anne Elliot's reflections are given through free indirect speech without quotation marks, but the implication is clearly on the lines of 'Anne wondered how . . .' The reader is given an insight into her consciousness that is the fictional equivalent of the dramatic soliloquy, yet the narrative voice remains in command (compare the artificiality of the effect obtained by another soliloquizing heroine, Hardy's Eustacia Vye in *The Return of the Native*, Bk V, Ch 7 of which offers a good example). Present-tense verbs move into the past, and *our* and *my* become *their* and *her*. This last instance well illustrates Ullmann's comment that free indirect speech 'supersedes the borderline between narrative and inner speech, so that the two imperceptibly merge into one another'.

It is now clear that free indirect speech offers the novelist the opportunity to combine some of the separate advantages of both the direct and the indirect forms. Pointing out that it 'has some features in common with both of the orthodox types', Ullmann enumerates the following as among its more usual characteristics.[8] (Although he is, in the discussion referred to, concerned with French style, most of his account applies with equal force to English usages.)

[1] Transposition of verbs: as in indirect speech, if the narrative is in the past tense, the verbs will change, the present becoming the preterite, the preterite the pluperfect, etc, though it is possible to find exceptions to this.

[2] Transposition of pronouns: again as in indirect speech, first and second persons change to third.

[3] Absence of subordination: each sentence appears as an independent unit, not a subordinate clause, so that there is no 'key verb' on which it is syntactically dependent.

[4] Preservation of such 'emotive elements' as questions, exclamations, interjections, colloquial language, slang and vulgar terms, together with an attempt to imitate 'the inflexions and intonations of the speaking voice'.

Of these, the most important in terms of literary effect is the last, offering as it does almost unlimited possibilities of stylistic variety without the necessity of transition to the sometimes cumbrous and uneconomical mode of direct speech.

Later nineteenth-century novelists were not slow to discover the usefulness of the free indirect form. Another quotation from *Edwin Drood* (1870) will reveal the smoothness and pace it can permit:

> . . . she feels it much more to the purpose to encourage him. And she does encourage him. } *narrative*
>
> He will write to her?
> He will write to her every alternate day, and tell her all his adventures. } *free indirect speech*
> Does he send clothes on in advance of him?
>
> "My dear Helena, no. Travel like a pilgrim, with wallet and staff . . . and here is my staff!" } *direct speech*
>
> He hands it to her; she makes the same remark as Mr Crisparkle, that it is very heavy; and gives it back to him, asking what wood it is? Ironwood. } *narrative; indirect speech; free indirect speech (or free direct speech?)*

This dialogue between Neville Landless and his sister includes within a few lines both direct and indirect as well as free indirect (and perhaps free direct) speech. (The free indirect speech shows in this case the changes of person, but not the changes of tense, already noted as customary.) It achieves an admirable briskness by the omission of explicit indications of speaker and by free movement between different modes of speech-presentation. Furthermore, it contrives to present dialogue without the abdication of the narrator's role as story-teller: although the 'voices' of Neville and Helena are given a hearing, it is the authorial 'voice' which remains dominant throughout.

It has already been implied that a substantial task of analysis and definition remains to be undertaken in the field of categories of speech-presentation, and that it may be almost as misleading to limit the number to four (including the 'free' forms) as to follow traditional grammarians in restricting it to two.[9] There would seem to be a number of constructions, by no means rare in works of literature, for which a precise and generally-accepted terminology is lacking. Nor is the matter solely one of linguistic interest, for the examples quoted in this chapter (and both examples and authors might have been multiplied many times) surely show that the writer who has at his disposal a wide range of modes of presenting speech is capable of achieving effects of unusual subtlety and flexibility in the context of a literary work.

Three special cases of speech in fiction – to use the term 'speech' for a moment in an extended but still legitimate sense – remain to be considered: interior monologue, the first-person narrative, and the epistolary novel. None of these is covered by the traditional definition of dialogue, yet all have a relationship to speech that helps to determine in many cases their specific stylistic qualities.

Dujardin, whose authority as a theorist is backed by his experience as a practitioner (he cites Joyce's acknowledgment that his *Les Lauriers sont Coupés* 'created' interior monologue), offers a definition of the first of these. He describes it as 'unheard and unspoken speech, by means of which a character expresses his innermost thoughts, as closely as possible to the unconscious, and independently of any logical organization, that is, by means of sentences reduced to the syntactic minimum'.[10] His contention, in other words, is that interior monologue is recognizable by its purpose – to reflect what he calls 'thought in a nascent state' (*la pensée à l'état naissant*) – as well as by certain stylistic, and particularly syntactical, features. It can thus be treated as a special case of monologue, in which the thoughts are not only unspoken but not fully verbalized, at least according to the canons of normal discourse. Interior monologue proper seeks (according to Dujardin's definition) to suggest the quality of thought as being different

in important respects from that of utterance; and there are many monologues in fiction (those of Ralph Nickleby and Eustacia Vye have already
been referred to) which do not belong to this category but are simply normal speeches of some length which do not happen to have an audience.
Although the use of interior monologue is associated with the experimental novelists of the early twentieth century such as James Joyce and
Dorothy Richardson, a similar technique has been found occurring
intermittently and on a modest scale in certain earlier novelists, including
Fanny Burney and Fennimore Cooper; and some striking examples of
sentence-fragmentation, with the omission of many formal elements and
logical links, to suggest the confused and rapid processes of thought at
moments of emotional excitement, may be found in Jane Austen.

Instances of interior monologue are also encountered in Dickens, though
not so commonly as has sometimes been maintained. Harry Stone has
claimed that Dickens anticipates later novelists in many passages in which
he seeks to 'examine and represent the mind's flow and to recreate the immediacy of experience'.[11] To this it may be objected, however, that most
of the examples cited in support of Stone's claim can only be classed as
interior monologue by an unwarrantable stretching of the term. Such
characters as Jingle, Mrs Nickleby and Flora Finching, whose speech contains some interesting stylistic experimentation, speak only when addressing another character: monologues they may utter, but these are scarcely
'interior'. It is eccentrically structured discourse, rather than the mind's
ebb and flow, that Dickens is creating: such qualities as incompleteness and
inconsequentiality are not, after all, a monopoly of the silent mental processes. So that, for all its brilliance and originality, such a stylistic *tour de
force* as *Mrs Lirriper's Lodgings* remains stubbornly an *exterior* monologue.
Perhaps the nearest Dickens came to true interior monologue or 'stream
of consciousness' writing was at the end of his life, in the opening paragraph of *Edwin Drood*:

An ancient English Cathedral Tower? How can the ancient English ⌐Town
Cathedral Tower be here! The well-known massive grey square tower
of its old Cathedral? How can that be here! There is no spike of rusty
iron in the air, between the eye and it, from any point of the real prospect. What is the spike that intervenes, and who has set it up? Maybe
it is set up by the Sultan's orders for the impaling of a horde of Turkish
robbers, one by one. It is so, for cymbals clash, and the Sultan goes by
to his palace in long procession . . . Stay! Is the spike so low a thing as
the rusty spike on top of a post of an old bedstead that has tumbled

all awry? Some vague period of drowsy laughter must be devoted
to the consideration of this possibility.

Shaking from head to foot, the man whose scattered consciousness
has thus fantastically pieced itself together, at length rises . . .

The opening questions and exclamations announce this as something different from the impersonal narrative voice with which most Victorian
novels open; nor is it, evidently, a conventional autobiographical narrative, since the tense is the present. The non-finite constructions of the two
opening questions suggest a puzzlement that is at odds with the normal
assurance of narrative (as exemplified by, for example, the opening lines of
David Copperfield or *Little Dorrit*). The shifting and bewildered impressions – their status as reality or illusion is at first equivocal – take us
straight into the 'scattered consciousness' of the drugged Jasper as he
slowly emerges from his opium-induced sleep and attempts to identify his
surroundings. Perception of his actual surroundings merges with memories
(of the cathedral of which he is an official) and fantastic dreams, until the
emphatic 'Stay!' asserts the demands of the real world and signals the
waning power of the drug. Only in the final sentence of that first paragraph does the narrator begin to take over: what precedes it *might* be
taken as the unspoken thoughts of Jasper, though they are expressed in
something that is much more than the 'syntactic minimum' of Dujardin's
definition already quoted, and very different from the unpunctuated free
association of (say) Molly Bloom in *Ulysses*:

> Yes because he never did a thing like that before as ask to get his breakfast
> in bed with a couple of eggs since the *City Arms* hotel when he used to
> be pretending to be laid up with a sick voice doing his highness to make
> himself interesting to that old faggot Mrs Riordan that he thought he
> had a great leg of and she never left us a farthing all for masses for her-
> self and her soul greatest miser ever was . . .

The prose of the *Edwin Drood* passage shows a logical control, with its
material ordered in conventional patterns: Jasper's half-awake state interferes much less than Molly's with the completeness of the sentences or the
internal arrangement of their elements for rhetorical effect.

The term 'interior monologue' must, therefore, be used with considerable hesitation of nineteenth-century novelists in English. Of Joyce,
Virginia Woolf, and other twentieth-century writers, it can of course be
used much more confidently and precisely. Two quotations will suggest
some of its distinctive features:

Mrs Dalloway said she would buy the flowers herself.

For Lucy had her work cut out for her. The doors would be taken off their hinges; Rumpelmayer's men were coming. And then, thought Clarissa Dalloway, what a morning – fresh as if issued to children on a beach.

What a lark! What a plunge! For so it had always seemed to her, when, with a little squeak of the hinges, which she could hear now, she had burst open the French windows and plunged at Bourton into the open air. How fresh, how calm, stiller than this of course, the air was in the early morning; like the flap of a wave; the kiss of a wave; chill and sharp and yet (for a girl of eighteen as she then was) solemn, feeling as she did, standing there at the open window, that something awful was about to happen; looking at the flowers, at the trees with the smoke winding off them and the rooks rising, falling; standing and looking until Peter Walsh said, "Musing among the vegetables?" – was that it? – "I prefer men to cauliflowers" – was that it? He must have said it at breakfast one morning when she had gone out on to the terrace – Peter Walsh.   [*Mrs Dalloway*, 1925]

Virginia Woolf moves quickly, in the first two sentences of her novel (of which the opening passage is quoted), from ordinary indirect speech to a free form which conveys the heroine's thoughts without the distraction of an introductory verb of thinking. The resemblance to free indirect speech extends to the modification of pronouns and verb-tenses. What this movement means is that narrative (in the opening sentence) immediately gives place to speech – or, more precisely, unspoken thoughts – with what appears to be direct access on the reader's part to the mental processes of the novel's central character. The reader's awareness that, from the second sentence onwards, he is being offered Clarissa Dalloway's thoughts rather than further reflections by the impersonal narrative voice is strengthened by an occasional reminder (*cf* the explicit 'thought Clarissa Dalloway' in the fourth sentence), and, more pervasively, by the colloquial flavour of such words and expressions as 'had her work cut out', 'What a lark!', and (shortly after the passage quoted) 'awfully dull' and 'grumpiness', which all belong to the idiom of spontaneous speech rather than to the more formal language of narrative style. Lexically as well as grammatically, therefore, interior monologue style is distinguishable from that of other portions of the novel. The fact that most of the passage consists of interior monologue does not mean, however, that the authorial voice is entirely silent: apart from 'thought Clarissa Dalloway', which reminds the reader of the mode employed, as a broadcasting station will remind listeners periodically of its own identity, such explanatory phrases as 'which she could hear now' and 'as she then was' surely constitute an interruption of the character's thoughts by a narrator conscious of the responsibilities of that function. A great advantage of this technique is that different elements may be combined without the formality of the usual indications of speech or thought and the often awkward transitions from one 'system' to another.

For writing of this kind, aiming to catch the undirected and inconsequential quality of casual thought, the traditional English sentence, with its hierarchical internal organization of main and subordinate clauses, would be quite inappropriate. We find at some points an absence of coordinating or subordinating elements which would normally be provided, as in 'The doors would be taken off their hinges; Rumpelmayer's men were coming'. The long and apparently unshaped sentence, with a low degree of predictability, is also found, as in the penultimate sentence quoted ('How fresh ... was that it?'): such features as repetition, self-interruption and self-questioning belong more obviously to spoken than to written prose and seem intended to reinforce the impression of the spontaneous flow of thought. Yet the looseness, the casualness, the absence of pattern due to recollections arising haphazardly, are more apparent than real, and the impression referred to can be seen on analysis to be achieved by a syntax which shows a considerable degree of control. Consider the structure of the sentence just referred to ('How fresh ...'). A selection and rearrangement of its main elements will best show its structural qualities:

{ *How fresh,*
{ *How calm* ... the air was in the early morning;
{ like *the flap of a wave;*
{   *the kiss of a wave;*
{ *chill* and
{ *sharp* and yet ...
{ *solemn,*
{ *feeling* as she did,
{ *standing* there at the open window ...
{ *looking* { *at the flowers*
{   { *at the trees* ...
{ *standing* and
{ *looking* until Peter Walsh said,

{ "Musing among the vegetables?" – *was that it?* –
{ "I prefer men to cauliflowers" – *was that it?*

This is indeed heavily patterned prose, hardly less so than that of Gibbon or Pater, with an extensive use of repetition of verbal structures, of balance and antithesis, of groupings in twos and threes, and with the arrangement of units of different lengths to create a definite climax. Beneath the suggestion of a free flow of thoughts and memories, echoing at random in the mind (echoes mimed in the sentence by the repetition of sounds as well as words and phrases), a strong principle of ordering is at work, resulting in a rhythmic quality which makes such prose closer to free verse than to the fictional prose of (say) H. G. Wells or Arnold Bennett. Again, therefore, the alliance to natural speech is illusory: for all its apparent spontaneity, such prose possesses an *organized* quality which makes it essentially remote from truly spontaneous discourse.

Another passage from *Ulysses* (1922), superficially very different, exhibits a similar mingling of diverse elements:

He walked cheerfully towards the mosque of the baths. Remind you of a mosque, redbaked bricks, the minarets. College sports today I see. He eyed the horseshoe poster over the gate of college park: cyclist doubled up like a cod in a pot. Damn bad ad. Now if they had made it round like a wheel. Then the spokes: sports, sports, sports: and the hub big: college. Something to catch the eye.

There's Hornblower standing at the porter's lodge. Keep him on hands: might take a turn in there on the nod. How do you do, Mr Hornblower? How do you do, sir?

Heavenly weather, really. If life was always like that. Cricket weather. Sit around under sunshades. Over after over. Out. They can't play it here. Duck for six wickets. Still Captain Buller broke a window in the Kildare street club with a slog to square leg. Donnybrook fair more in their line. And the skulls we were acracking when M'Carthy took the floor. Heatwave. Won't last . . .

The novelist shifts unfussily from narrative (in the first sentence quoted) to inner speech, and (shortly after this passage) back again, with a brief incursion into direct speech. We may enquire how the shift is signalled to the reader, in the absence of (for instance) attributions to speaker or graphological indications of speech. It has been pointed out that in such passages there is a marked contrast between the linguistic features of the narrative portions and the monologues.[12] The former employ a formal grammar and vocabulary, with 'complete sentences' of the traditional varieties (witness the first sentence quoted, and the fourth as far as the colon), whilst the latter are often verbless or incomplete ('Heatwave. Won't last.') and include the shortened forms of verbs (*There's, can't*) and other colloquial items such as 'I see' and the final 'really'. What has happened is that the conventional external signs of distinction between speech (or speech-thought) and narrative have been rejected, their purpose being adequately served by a contrast in stylistic modes which the reader is likely to respond to unconsciously even if he does not consciously observe it.

Both the first-person narrative and the novel in letters have a history as long as that of the novel itself, and both represent narrative methods which can (but in practice do not always) derive some of their stylistic flavour from speech. Since the confessional memoir was an important tributary stream of early fictional development, it is not surprising that Defoe's *Moll Flanders* (1722) – to take a familiar early example of the first-person novel – should be cast in this form. The influence of spoken language upon Defoe's style, and not only upon the dialogue passages, is striking: the recent suggestion that some of his material may have been taken down in shorthand in a Newgate cell from Moll's namesake and prototype may help to explain this feature.[13] The original title-page announces the story as 'Written from her own Memorandums', and in the cause of promoting this fiction Defoe seems to have taken some pains to abandon his normal competent journalistic prose (as evinced in his non-fictional writings of the same period) in favour of a style which achieves a racy colloquialism by borrowing many of the characteristics of spoken prose:

> It was at Colchester, in Essex, that those people left me; and I have a notion in my head that I left them there (that is, that I hid myself and would not go any farther with them), but I am not able to be particular in that account; only this I remember, that being taken up by some of the parish officers of Colchester, I gave an account that I came into the town with the gypsies, but that I would not go any farther with them, and that so they had left me, but whither they were gone that I knew not, for though they sent round the country to inquire after them, it seems that they could not be found.

The loose structure with the frequent use of coordinating conjunctions in preference to subordinate clauses, like the breaking off to explain a point more fully (marked by the parentheses), seems to offer a guarantee of the authenticity of Defoe's material: there is fluency but a calculated absence of polish and economy, thereby convincingly suggesting an informant anxious to give a complete and accurate account and searching her memory, not always successfully, for the events of half a century earlier. In the more dramatic passages, such as Moll's accounts of her various crimes, dialogue within the narrative is used to good effect:

> While I sat here, I heard the woman in the bar say, "Are they all gone in the five?" which was the box I sat in, and the boy said, "Yes". "Who fetched the tankard away?" says the woman. "I did," says another boy. "That's it," pointing, it seems, to another tankard, which he had fetched from another box by mistake; or else it must be that the rogue forgot that he had not brought it in, which certainly he had not.

If this conversation never actually took place, one feels that it might well have done so. Yet the colloquial element is not confined to the dialogue but permeates the narrative too, such an expression as 'the rogue' serving to remind us of the reminiscing voice behind the written narrative. The narrator is distanced from the events she recalls in time but not in emotional attitudes, her memories often seeming to come to life as she is in the act of speaking of them, and frequently in mid-sentence – an impression reinforced by the frequent tense-shifts from past to present and back again.

The claim of the first-person novel to be considered as sustained speech or monologue should not, of course, be exaggerated. Even when the fiction is presented, as in *Wuthering Heights*, wholly or largely as a personal narrative, the attempt to suggest the particular qualities of the speaking voices may be a very limited one. Consider, for example, the often highly literary idiom of Marlow's narrative in Conrad's *Heart of Darkness*. There is clearly considerable variation possible in the relationship of such narratives to speech, and the 'voice' of Moll Flanders is closer to eighteenth-century speech than the 'voice' of Jane Eyre is to that of the early Victorian period: even our imperfect knowledge of the colloquial language of past periods will perhaps allow such broad generalizations.

Some novelists have also been conscious of the limitations of, as well as the technical difficulties of narrative method created by, a single narrative voice. Prominent among these limitations is the stylistic one of the tedium inherent in any markedly individual style pursued at length without relief. The novelist thus faces a dilemma; if he makes his narrator a character with a highly individual 'voice', he runs the risk of lack of stylistic variety; but a neutral or non-idiosyncratic manner will place a severe limitation on the possibilities of stylistic interest. Dickens went some way towards solving this problem in *Bleak House*, where a first-person and a third-person narrative, alternating irregularly, are combined in almost exactly equal proportions. (Their stylistic differences are discussed in Chapter 6 below.) Wilkie Collins's *The Moonstone* makes ingenious use of a whole series of narrators in turn, with appropriate stylistic contrasts; and Conrad's *Lord Jim* places a neutral, third-person framework round the narrative of Marlow, which itself incorporates a number of minor narratives with a variety of individual 'voices'. There is the possibility of variation, too, in the status of the narrator, who is usually but need not necessarily be a central figure in the action. The different degrees of impartiality represented by Lockwood and Ellen Dean, who share the narrator's task in *Wuthering Heights*, aid plausibility by providing a pair of links between the reader and the world of the novel. Where the narrator is also the hero, as in *Roderick Random* and *David Copperfield* and *Catcher in the Rye*, the choice of narrative material is largely dictated by the hero's participation; but the use of a minor character as narrator can result in the need for a good deal of ingenuity in order that episodes can be recounted in the words of an eye-witness. (In Chapter 30 of *Wuthering Heights*, for instance, Lockwood learns of a conversation that has taken place between Heathcliff and Catherine only because the servant Zillah has happened to be present and has passed it on to Nelly, who in turn retails it to Lockwood – a clumsy sacrifice on the altar of first-person narrative.)

Finally, there is some justification for briefly considering the epistolary novel as a special case of fictional speech. The notion of the familiar letter as a substitute for conversation – as 'talking on paper' or *sermo absentis ad absentem* – is a long-established one.[14] As Jane Austen wrote to her sister Cassandra:

> I have now attained the true art of letter-writing, which we are always told, is to express on paper exactly what one would say to the same person by word of mouth . . .[15]

At the same time, whilst an informal letter-style is likely to occupy a position somewhere between speech and ordinary written prose, its differences from the former are usually obvious enough. Part of the intention of such a letter may be to provide the illusion of an intimate (though one-sided) gossip, and a prolonged correspondence may resemble a protracted slow-motion dialogue; but even the most spontaneously-composed letters, written in haste with a minimum of calculation, are a long way from being a transcript of speech. Tom Moore observed that Byron's habit of answering letters immediately gave his replies 'all the aptitude and freshness of replies in conversation',[16] but one does not have to study the letters

very closely to detect in them a polish, precision and economy of statement, together with a conscious calculation of literary effect, that make
them quite different from the unrehearsed speech of even the most brilliant conversationalist. When they are casual and informal, indeed, this
may be taken to be part of the writer's intention. Both Byron and Jane
Austen are the heirs of an eighteenth-century tradition of letter-writing,
which is itself related to the practice of conversation as a social art in that
period, as well as to the epistolary mode in which so much of its fiction is
cast. In fiction, the letter has an ancestry that stretches back a long way
before the first important example, Richardson's *Pamela*, and it has been
estimated that some two hundred works of 'letter fiction' appeared between the Restoration and 1740.[17] After the extraordinary success of
Pamela, the epistolary novel gathered strength to become one of the dominant forms of fiction, especially feminine fiction, in the last quarter of the
eighteenth century. The tradition survives in Scott's *Redgauntlet* (1824)
and in other nineteenth-century novels by Galt, Lytton, Landor, and
others, as well as in such later popular successes as Bram Stoker's *Dracula*
(1897), Jean Webster's *Daddy-Long-Legs* (1912) and A. P. Herbert's
Topsy (1931).[18]

In this chapter, however, we can look only at a couple of examples. In
the great eighteenth-century epistolary novels, from *Clarissa* and *Grandi-
son* to *Humphry Clinker* and *Evelina*, the letter is the exclusive or principal
medium for conducting the narrative, and the effect is of a series of monologues, many of them springing from an immediate dramatic situation,
and some of them (like Byron's letters) displaying a carefully-contrived
spontaneity which Richardson and his followers felt to be one of the
supreme virtues of the medium.

In the 1759 Preface to *Clarissa*, Richardson refers to the '*instantaneous*
Descriptions and Reflections' and the 'affecting Conversations' of his
novel – 'many of them', as he adds, 'written in the dialogue or dramatic
way'. The language of such passages is often influenced by speech, although it is the written style of the characters that is in question; and the
reader's attention is continually being drawn to them in the act of writing
their long and detailed letters, which may be regarded as equivalent to the
act of speaking. Like a speech, a letter in the process of composition may
be interrupted by dramatic action – a knock at the door or some other
interruption – or by 'instantaneous' observations, as in *Pamela*:

So, so! where will this end? – Mrs Jewkes has been with me from him,
and she says, I must get out of the house this moment . . . There is, I see,

the chariot drawn out, the horses too, the grim Colbrand going to get on horseback. What will be the end of all this?

Fielding's satire, in *Shamela*, was quick to ridicule this overworked but not unrealistic device:

> Mrs Jervis and I are just in Bed, and the Door unlocked; if my Master should come – Odsbobs! I hear him just coming in at the Door. You see I write in the present Tense ...

But later novelists were not discouraged from imitating Richardson's method and striving (usually in vain) for even more ambitious dramatic effects. *The Precipitate Choice* (1772) offers the following sample of the epistolary art from a distracted husband:

> Oh! my Lord, what have I done! – My wife, my adored wife, my Isabella, lies murdered by my side, murdered by me. No, she is not yet dead, she grasps my hand – she strives to speak ...[19]

Absurd as such examples are, they serve to illustrate the close resemblance of fictional letters to dramatic monologues.

A short passage from *Clarissa* may be referred to as illustrating the theatrical element in Richardson's fiction and, particularly, the closeness of his letters at many points to speech, or at least to dramatic dialogue. I refer to three letters written by Lovelace to Belford and all dated 9 June. In the first of these (headed 'Friday Morning, past Two o'clock') Lovelace expresses his exhilaration as Clarissa moves unknowingly into his clutches, his emotion being expressed through exclamations, imperatives and rhetorical questions, as well as by a jauntily colloquial diction (Clarissa is a 'dear juggler' and a 'sweet rogue'). In addition to what the letter conveys through Lovelace's own epistolary 'voice', there are two other elements which add variety: the record of his speeches to a servant apparently uttered simultaneously with the writing of the letter, voice and hand going together, and transcripts of two other letters within the parent letter, written in contrasting styles: one from his semi-literate servant William Summers ('This is to sertifie your Honner ...'), the other in the stately formal prose, heavy with abstractions, of Clarissa. His next letter, written a few hours later, reports recent action in more obviously dramatic form:

> And here, supposing my narrative of the dramatic kind, ends Act the First. And now begins
>
> ACT II
>
>   *Scene:* Hampstead Heath, continued.
>
>   Enter my Rascal.

The ensuing dialogue is interspersed with stage-directions, and the collo-quial idiom of the servant is stressed by the italicization of words and phrases ('she was *mortal* jealous of him', etc).[20] A third letter follows which again makes extensive use of dialogue. Even so brief a summary suggests the variety of which the epistolary method, in Richardson's hands, is capable. Not only does Lovelace write in a passionate and excla-matory style which seems to have his own speech pressing upon it: he also mimics (consistently enough with his skill at deception of all kinds) the voices of others, so that substantial stretches of the novel resemble a drama-tic script.

As a final example, Smollett's *Humphry Clinker* (1771) shows that the epistolary method, like dialogue, is a rich source of stylistic variety and contrast. At many points the reader is given two or more accounts of the same scene or episode, in which the interest springs from the contrast in styles and in characters thus revealed. In this way, Matt Bramble's sour account of Vauxhall is followed by his niece's gushing praise for the same place, her enthusiasm being itself later satirized by similar sentiments from the less skilful pen of Win Jenkins. In epistolary fiction, the speech-element is not restricted to the dialogue quoted in the course of the letters, but is apt to permeate much of the writing which appears at first sight to be narrative or descriptive. Moreover, the sustained correspondences which are conducted between various pairs of characters in *Clarissa* and (one-sidedly) in *Humphry Clinker* can usefully be regarded as extended and specialized modes of conversation.

Notes

1 M. Gregory, 'Aspects of Varieties Differentiation', *Journal of Linguistics*, 3, 1967, 193.

2 G. Sherburn, 'Samuel Richardson's Novels and the Theatre: A Theory Sketched', *Philological Quarterly*, 41, 1962, 325. See also B. W. Downs, *Richardson*, London, 1928, 97; L. Hughes, 'Theatrical Convention in Richardson: Some Observations on a Novelist's Technique', *Restoration and Eighteenth-Century Literature: Essays in Honor of Alan Dugald McKillop*, Chicago, 1963, 201–9.

3 *Cf* W. Raleigh, *The English Novel*, 1894, 142.

4 B. Blackstone, *Indirect Speech: its Principles and Practice*, 1962, 1.

5 *Cf* G. L. Schuelke, '"Slipping" in Indirect Discourse', *American Speech*, 33, 1958, 90–8.

6 *Cf* L. Glauser, *Die erlebte Rede im englischen Roman des 19. Jahrhunderts*, Zurich, 1948, which examines the use of free indirect speech by eight nineteenth-century English novelists. See also M. Lips, *Le Style Indirect Libre*, Paris, 1926; S. Ullmann, *Style in the French Novel*, Cambridge, 1957, Ch 2.

7 *Cf* N. Page, 'Categories of Speech in *Persuasion*', *Modern Language Review*, 64, 1969, 734–41.

8 S. Ullmann, op cit, 97–9.

9 *Cf* M. Gregory, 'Old Bailey Speech in *A Tale of Two Cities*', *Review of English Literature*, 6, 1965, 55.

10 E. Dujardin, *Le Monologue Intérieur*, Paris, 1931, 58–9 (my translation). See also D. Bickerton, 'Modes of Interior Monologue – a Formal Definition', *Modern Language Quarterly*, 28, 1967, 229–39.

11 H. Stone, 'Dickens and Interior Monologue', *Philological Quarterly*, 38, 1959, 52.

12 The passage is discussed by J. Spencer, 'A Note on the "Steady Monologuy of the Interiors"', *Review of English Literature*, 6, 2, 1965, 35–41.

13 *Cf* G. Howson, 'Who Was Moll Flanders?', *Times Literary Supplement*, 18 January 1968, 63–4.

14 Pope's 'concept of a good letter was that it was "talking on paper" to friends' (G. Sherburn, *The Correspondence of Alexander Pope*, Oxford, 1956, I, x).

15 *Jane Austen's Letters*, ed R. W. Chapman, 1952, 102.

16 Quoted by J. D. Jump, 'Byron's Letters', *Essays and Studies of the English Association*, 1968, 63.

17 R. A. Day, *Told in Letters: Epistolary Fiction Before Richardson*, Ann Arbor, Michigan, 1966, 2.

18 For fuller information, see G. F. Singer, *The Epistolary Novel*, New York, 1933; F. G. Black, *The Epistolary Novel in the Late Eighteenth Century*, Eugene, 1940.

19 Quoted by J. M. S. Tompkins, *The Popular Novel in England, 1770–1800*, 1932, 334.

20 According to W. P. Uhrström, 'If we wish to study the spoken language of (Richardson's) time we can hardly find a better source than his works' (*Studies on the Language of Samuel Richardson*, Upsala, 1907, 3).

Further references

D. Bickerton, 'James Joyce and the Development of Interior Monologue', *Essays in Criticism*, 18, 1968, 32–46.

D. Cohn, 'Narrated Monologue: Definition of a Fictional Style', *Comparative Literature*, 18, 1966, 97–112.

B. Fehr, 'Substitutionary Narrative and Description', *English Studies*, 20, 1938, 97–107.

G. Hough, 'Narrative and Dialogue in Jane Austen', *Critical Quarterly*, 12, 1970, 201–29.

C. Jones, 'Varieties of Speech Presentation in Conrad's *The Secret Agent*', *Lingua*, 20, 1968, 162–76.

B. Romberg, *Studies in the Narrative Technique of the First-person Novel*, Lund, 1962.

P. Stevick, 'Stylistic Energy in the Early Smollett', *Studies in Philology*, 64, 1967, 712–19.

Chapter 3

Speech and character: dialect

The dialogue in a novel is, as we have seen, multifunctional: it can serve to further plot, to develop character, to describe setting or atmosphere, to present a moral argument or a discussion on cabbages or kings, or to perform any combination of these purposes. Probably the most important, however, and certainly the most productive of interest and variety, is the presentation and development of character. Earlier examples have shown that the importance of dialogue in relation to other elements is not a constant, nor does it always function in the same way. Where character-presentation is concerned, it may exist mainly as a supplement to the author's or narrator's direct exposition – an illustration of points already made in general terms. Thus, in *Tom Jones*, Fielding habitually offers the reader an account of a character in his own authorial voice *before* introducing speech and action. The opening chapter of *Pride and Prejudice* reverses this method: Jane Austen's commentary on Mr and Mrs Bennet is given only *after* the reader has had the opportunity of forming his own impressions from a brief but revealing exchange of speeches. Differently again, in much modern fiction dialogue becomes a substitute for explicit analysis of character: in Hemingway's stories, for example, the dramatic method often dispenses with commentary entirely and throws the burden of character-assessment upon the reader without any opportunity of measuring his judgment against that of the author.

Within the dialogue itself, differences may exist in the variety of modes of speech employed: in their range, the qualities they suggest, and the means by which they are differentiated. Trollope, according to Geoffrey Tillotson, tends to make most of his characters speak with a single voice, his own;[1] Scott uses at least two languages, formal English and Scots vernacular; and Dickens exhibits an astonishing diversity of styles, individualized in many different ways. Very broadly, speech-characteristics may be said to work in two directions, either identifying the character with some recognizable social or regional or other class, or distinguishing him from his fellows as a unique individual. And, though our concern is with literary conventions, it is worth saying that this has a rough correspondence with the characteristics of real-life speech, since we constantly, on the evidence of the spoken language, both classify those we meet according to such loose categories as 'middle-class' and 'north-country', and, as we grow more familiar with their speech, acknowledge certain features as particular to the individual.

Speech, then, offers two kinds of information – or may do so if the writer chooses to use it in this way. The first works outwards to show an affinity between the user and some identifiable group, actual or conventional; the second works inwards to denote individuality or even eccentricity. These may for convenience be referred to as group and individual features, or, more briefly, as dialect and idiolect. (Strictly speaking, of course, an idiolect may incorporate certain dialect features as part of the sum of characteristics, some of them widespread, but adding up to a unique combination.) This chapter and the one that follows are devoted, respectively, to these two aspects of characterization through speech. *Dialect* will be used as an inclusive term to cover regional, social and occupational varieties. There is, naturally, much merging of these categories: Cockney, for instance, was and is both a regional and a social dialect. And a single character may well exhibit evidence of membership of more than one group, as well as possessing distinctively individual speech-traits, so that a certain amount of dissection of a writer's total purpose is necessary if these various facets are to be discussed systematically.

Most of what follows relates to the conventions and techniques adopted by novelists in their use of dialects. What needs also to be taken into account, however, is the nature of the reader's response to the representation in fiction of different dialects. This response is likely to vary in a rather complex way according to the prevalent social attitudes and assumptions in different generations, as well as with the experience of the particular reader. In periods before widespread travel and promulgation of the spoken word by radio and other devices made a variety of accents and dialects familiar to nearly all, the writer using dialect words or indicating regional pronunciations ran the risk of mystifying his reader if his representation went very far in the direction of realism. The same reader might be better equipped to recognize a conventionalized literary dialect, such as Cockney became, since he might already have encountered it in his reading. Such a literary dialect would tend to develop a tradition of its own, and in the course of time would bear less and less resemblance to the living dialect with which it was associated. Furthermore, a written representation of dialect might convey very different things to different readers. Given an equal responsiveness to the printed word, consider what Cockney, for instance, might convey to a Cockney, a middle-class Londoner, a York-shireman who had never been to London, and an English-speaking foreigner. If we 'know' a dialect, either as a speaker or a practised listener, limited signals in a printed text, or even no signals at all within the dialogue itself, may be sufficient to enable us to reconstruct the appropriate phono-logical features and to 'hear' it as we read or to imitate it plausibly if we read the text aloud. If we are not familiar with the dialect, our response is likely to be quite different: we can only 'hear' (or read aloud) a kind of corrupt version of the dialect such as the indications within the text sug-gest. Another question of some importance concerns the associations aroused by dialect speech in a society in which, even before the novel emerged, it had come to be regarded as a marker of inferior status. One result was that its use in literature was long confined to comedy, or at least to a somewhat patronizing or complacent folksy humour. In spite of the example of Scott and Edgeworth (Scots and Irish dialects have in any case not carried the same social implications as English dialects) the comic tra-dition persisted until the mid-nineteenth century. When Mrs Gaskell used the Lancashire dialect in *Mary Barton* (1848) for serious purposes, she felt impelled to provide footnotes which not only glossed the meanings but cited parallels from Chaucer, the Prayer Book, and other highly esteemed early sources – thus making a frontal attack on the reader's social prejudice as well as his probable ignorance:

"Again", for against. "He that is not with me, he is ageyn me."
[*Wickliffe's Version*]

In discussing regional dialects, care must be taken not to stray across common frontiers into such neighbouring territories as slang and collo-quial speech, or uneducated speech. Words and expressions of these types may exist side by side with dialect forms, but they are not of course con-fined to any region and therefore call for separate treatment. Regional speech may be suggested in written dialogue by distinctive features of vocabulary or syntax and grammar, or by indications of non-standard pronunciation. Items of vocabulary may be quickly acquired by anyone with an alert ear and a limited acquaintance with dialect-speakers, or, even more easily, from dictionaries and glossaries of dialect words or from dialect literature. Grammar and syntax are, apart from the most obvious differences, less readily absorbed by the casual listener, and are used relatively little by writers. Much more extensively used are devices for suggesting non-standard pronunciation. By long-established tradition, any variant spelling may be interpreted as representing non-standard pronunciation, even where the spelling, as with *sez* and *tho'*, is a crude phonetic version of the standard pronunciation. Many of the examples which follow show these and other devices at work.

The full history of the use of regional dialects in English literature has yet to be written, and many of the piecemeal investigations which have been undertaken are of primarily philological or phonological interest. What will be attempted here is in no sense a comprehensive coverage, but a selective discussion of outstanding instances to illustrate some of the main uses and methods of dialect speech in the novel, and chosen with a view to their literary as well as their linguistic interest.

There is a long, though not a broad, tradition of dialect writing, usually for comic purposes, from the *Second Shepherds' Play* and the *Reeve's Tale*, through Shakespeare, to the eighteenth-century novelists.[2] For Fielding and Smollett, regional speech is symptomatic of lack of cultivation, if not downright boorishness. It may be no coincidence that *provincial*, as applied to manners and speech, in the sense 'lacking metropolitan polish', appears in the language in the same generation as *Tom Jones* and *Roderick Random*. In a London-based literary culture, provinciality becomes equated with inferiority. Fielding's Squire Western, whose name betrays his Somerset origins, is certainly provincial in the sense given to the word in Johnson's *Dictionary:* 'rude, unpolished'. His idiom is at times very broad, though his daughter Sophia shows no sign of her father's broad speech: it is still unthinkable that a heroine should speak in a manner associated primarily with comic effects.

> "Come, my lad," says Western, "d'off thy quoat and wash thy feace; for att in a devilish pickle, I promise thee. Come, come, wash thyself, and shat go huome with me; and we'l zee to vind thee another quoat."
> [*Tom Jones*, v, 12]

This is probably, to a significant extent, a literary dialect rather than a record based on direct observation, such orthographic features as the substitution of *z* for *s* and *v* for *f* (representing the voicing of unvoiced consonants) belonging to a stylized speech that may be designated 'Southern Rural'. It had been used by dramatists long before Fielding, who, as an experienced playwright, was no doubt familiar with stage dialect of this kind. (Ben Jonson's *A Tale of a Tub* (1633), for example, includes a comic countryman whose *zay* and *vace* belong to the same tradition as

Western's *zee* and *vind*.³) At moments of heartiness or anger, the dialect is strongly marked. In more sentimental mood, however, it is considerably less obtrusive, and in passages such as the following tends to come and go somewhat unpredictably:

"Why wout ask, Sophy?" cries he, "when dost know I had rather hear thy voice than the musick of the best pack of dogs in England. – Hear thee, my dear little girl! I hope I shall hear thee as long as I live; for if I was ever to lose that pleasure, I would not gee a brass varden to live a moment longer. Indeed, Sophy, you do not know how I love you, indeed you don't, or you never could have run away and left your poor father, who hath no other joy, no other comfort upon earth, but his little Sophy."   [*Tom Jones*, XVI, 2]

The expression 'gee a brass varden' stands out like a signpost to remind the reader that this is dialect speech, but it clearly suits the novelist to play down the dialect element when his intention is not primarily comic. In other words, dialect is a variable dependent on the demands of fictional situation rather than on the probable behaviour of an actual speaker. The other significant aspect of Fielding's dialogue is the use of variant spellings of ordinary English words – *feace* for *face*, *quoat* for *coat* – to suggest regional pronunciation: it is by this means, rather than, for example, by the use of dialect words and phrases, that the flavour of Western's speech is created. The reason is one of intelligibility: Fielding has no intention of baffling the reader, who is given only so much as seems easily tolerable. In both these respects, Fielding's example sets a pattern for many later novelists.

In the speech of Win Jenkins in *Humphry Clinker*, Smollett fashioned a more intricate and interesting comic idiolect, brilliantly successful in the novel but demonstrably not taken from the life. Win is a Welsh lady's maid who has never left her native Monmouthshire until she sets out with the Bramble family on their tour of England and Scotland; but, as W. A. Boggs has shown,⁴ the language of her letters turns out on analysis to be an extraordinary polyglot of diverse elements: Welsh English, Standard English, Cockney, a variety of Midland and Southern dialects, and Lowland Scots. It seems inconceivable that the speech of any individual, much less one with Win's background, should be such a ragbag of different components, and it is clear that Smollett has not hesitated to ransack the comic resources of any variety of English known to him for linguistic features which add to the richness and humour of Win's language. In the process he has, of course, shown little concern either for consistency or for the possibility that the linguistically alert reader might be disconcerted by his incongruities.

The example of Fielding and Smollett did not meet with universal approval. Reviewing a now-forgotten novel in the *Monthly Review* in 1784, a critic commented that 'Readers of taste will be disgusted at descriptions which enter too minutely into vulgar scenes, and at dialogues which are degraded by the cant of provincial speech'.[5] Evidently the prevailing 'doctrine of correctness' entailed a ban on non-standard usages, with a consequent impoverishing for many novelists of the resources of dialogue.

With Sir Walter Scott, however, a new dimension enters into the use of regional dialects in fiction. Behind the dialogue of the Waverley Novels lies the poetic theory of Wordsworth (who is referred to in the Advertisement to *The Antiquary* (1816)) regarding the dignity of rustic speech and its suitability for literary use. A few years earlier, John Jamieson had written, in his preface to the *Etymological Dictionary of the Scottish Language* (1808), that 'The peasantry are the living depositories of the ancient language of every country'; and Scott turned to the vernacular in no spirit of curiosity or condescension, but with a conviction that it constituted a worthy vehicle for the expression of the highest emotions and moral ideas. There is a moving passage in Lockhart's *Life* which reports a conversation in which Scott emphatically asserted the nobility of humble speech: 'I assure you', he remarked, 'I have heard higher sentiments from the lips of poor *uneducated* men and women . . . than I ever yet met with out of the pages of the Bible'. A work such as *The Heart of Midlothian* (1818), therefore, represents a significant change of direction in the novel, not only in its homely heroine and its stress on the dignity of humble life, but in its use of dialect speech for purposes no longer exclusively comic and eccentric, but heroic and even tragic. Scott writes not as a dialectologist or (as Dickens often does) a reporter, but as an insider with an intimate awareness of Scots speech as a living medium of daily communication and a deep respect for it as the outward token of qualities of character and conscience which aroused his admiration. We know from the evidence of his contemporaries that his own speech made use of many dialect words and expressions, and that he was capable of slipping at times into a broad Scots pronunciation. It is true that literary influences cannot be altogether discounted in considering the relationship of his dialogue to actual speech. As the remark reported by Lockhart suggests, he was aware of the extent of Biblical influence upon the natural speech of the unlearned and even the illiterate, and this element may be traced in some of his most effective dialogues. Another obvious and important influence was that of the traditional ballads: their vigour and directness, and their use of poetic idiom to express simple and heartfelt emotions, lend a strength to many passages. In the phrasing and rhythm of the following, for example, one surely catches the ballad note:

> "O, what wad I gie to be ten times waur, Jeanie!" was the reply –
> "what wad I gie to be cauld dead afore the ten o'clock bell the morn!
> And our father – but I am his bairn nae langer now – O, I hae nae
> friend left in the warld! – O, that I were lying dead at my mother's side,
> in Newbattle kirkyard!"   [*The Heart of Midlothian*, Ch 20]

Scott was, after all, folklorist as well as novelist; but his interest was not in the first place scholarly or antiquarian, and one rarely, in reading the Scots dialogue of these novels, has the sense that he is going far beyond what might be natural in such speakers – a community taking a conscious pride in its past, drawing its main influences from the Bible and from folk-idiom, and resistant alike to change and to outside influences.

At times Scott plays off the vernacular against the standard language, by no means to the disadvantage of the former. In Jeanie Deans's two interviews with the Duke of Argyle and with Queen Caroline (Chs 35, 37) her speech is a guarantee of her simplicity, integrity and lack of concern for outward forms which constitute true dignity and independence of spirit. When the Queen asks how she has travelled to London from Scotland,

> "Upon my foot mostly, madam," was the reply.
> "What, all that immense way upon foot? – How far can you walk in
> a day?"
> "Five and twenty miles and a bittock."
> "And a what?" said the Queen, looking towards the Duke of Argyle.
> "And about five miles more," replied the Duke.
> "I thought I was a good walker," said the Queen, "but this shames
> me sadly."
> "May your Leddyship never hae sae weary a heart, that ye canna be
> sensible of the weariness of the limbs!" said Jeanie.

The instinctive courtesy which enables Jeanie to dispense with the orthodox formalities transmutes her ignorance into a virtue. The last speech quoted underlines a dramatic effect that could hardly have been achieved had the two women, inhabitants of different worlds, not spoken different languages. The dialect element is not, however, a constant. Some idea of the degree of variation may be gained by comparing Jeanie's great speech in Chapter 37, in which she pleads for her sister's life, with the conversation she holds with Effie in prison (Ch 20). In the latter, the dialect is fairly strongly marked:

"What needs I tell ye ony thing about it," said Jeanie. "Ye may be sure he had ower muckle to do to save himsell, to speak lang or muckle about ony body beside."

In the course of a long speech, however, the need to provide frequent dialect-signals is less urgent. The following sentences appear in the middle of Jeanie's speech in Chapter 37, which has some claim to be considered the climactic point of the novel:

". . . Save an honest house from dishonour, and an unhappy girl, not eighteen years of age, from an early and dreadful death! Alas! it is not when we sleep soft and wake merrily ourselves, that we think on other people's sufferings . . ."

Before and after this quotation, reminders that Jeanie is speaking dialect have been provided; but the ease of reading a long speech – and perhaps, given Scott's methods of composition, the speed of writing it – renders a uniform imposition of dialect words and non-standard spellings not only unnecessary but undesirable. What distinguishes these sentences from those of the English-speaking characters, however, is their distinctive syntax and rhythm, the urgent imperative of 'Save' and the echoing of 'honest . . . dishonour', together with the hint of folk idiom in 'sleep soft and wake merrily'.

If Jeanie Deans represents the best of Scott's dialogue, the worst is not difficult to find. Characters speaking standard English are often as stilted and verbose as the dialect-speakers are vigorous and expressive. In the same novel, almost any speech by Staunton is stiff with abstract nouns and cloudy with hackneyed expressions: in a few lines in Chapter 33, a case terminates favourably, tidings are fatal, resolutions are instantly taken, the utmost haste is made. At such times, Scott writes dialogue like a tired civil servant composing a formal communication. He has obviously not *heard* the words he sets down, and the dialogue is not sufficiently differentiated from the narrative style (itself often verbose and turgid) to provide any adequate illusion of the spoken language. Failure to attend to the sound of his prose, and to ensure that it reads aloud well, is indeed one of the reasons why Scott, writing rapidly and revising little, so often writes sentences that grate unpleasantly on the ear of a reader who cares for this element:

Possessed of this *information*, and with a mind agitated by the most gloomy *apprehensions*, Butler now joined the Captain, and obtained from him with some difficulty a sight of the *examinations*. These, with a few *questions* to the elder of the prisoners, soon confirmed the most dreadful of Butler's *anticipations*. We give the heads of the *information*, without descending into minute details. [*My italics*]

This, from the last chapter of the novel, when Scott was presumably anxious to get his task over, is painfully clumsy with its superfluity of similar-sounding words: even more than the stilted dialogue referred to, it is lifeless because it is irredeemably alien from speech; and one might risk the generalization that Scott writes well, in both dialogue and non-dialogue passages, only when he is conscious of the pressure of the spoken language behind his prose. For all this, his achievement was substantial, not only in the new status given to dialect, but, more widely, in the greater importance assumed by dialogue in his novels. As Ian Jack has written, 'It has been given to few men to effect so great a revolution of taste in the response of readers to a language. This is the root of Scott's greatness. It is by their speeches that he creates every one of his most successful characters.'[6]

Among Scott's successors in the regional novel (and to ignore chronology for the moment), some of the finest dialect writing is to be found in R. L. Stevenson's *Weir of Hermiston* (1896) – in, for example, the interview between Hermiston and his son in the third chapter. Hermiston is avowedly modelled on Lord Braxfield, whom Stevenson elsewhere describes as 'the last judge on the Scotch bench to employ the pure Scotch idiom', and the irreconcilable difference in temperaments between father and son is dramatically underlined by their use of, respectively, a broad and vigorous vernacular and a standard English which, by contrast, appears bloodless and emasculated. As David Daiches has pointed out, in the course of the scene Hermiston's speech becomes more markedly Scots, whilst Archie's remains that of one who has failed to live up to the traditions of his family. Later in the same book a similar contrast is to be found in the dialogues between Archie and Kirstie: only at one point does Archie, 'profoundly moved', lapse into 'the broad Scots' (Ch 8), thus setting aside for a moment the social barrier between master and housekeeper under the pressure of strong feelings.

Though a greater novelist than Scott or Stevenson, Dickens had neither their sense of the living relationship of dialect to history and tradition, nor (except perhaps for Cockney) a deep and instinctive feeling for its rhythms and idioms. In the earlier novels, dialect is used somewhat perfunctorily to provide local colour; in *Nicholas Nickleby* (1839), for instance, Yorkshire speech is presented by a reporter with an alert and retentive ear – he had visited the area briefly at the end of 1837 to gather material for his novel – but no real feeling for its distinctive quality. John Browdie is a minor character hardly developed beyond a regional type, that of the rough-spoken but warm-hearted Yorkshireman. His speech contains few dialect words or expressions; instead, Dickens relies for his effect upon the render-ing of pronunciation through variant spellings, concentrating on the broad vowel-sounds: *weel* (will), *loove* (love), etc. Nor is he always con-sistent: *heerd* and *heard* occur in the same passage. The East Anglian speech of *David Copperfield* is interesting in a different way, since it has been shown that Dickens here relies substantially upon a printed source, Moor's *Suffolk Words and Phrases* (1823).[7] This probably explains the striking fact that, although Dickens knew even less of East Anglian speech at first-hand than he did of Yorkshire speech (he had spent only a few hours in Yarmouth, home of the Peggottys, whilst on a tour of the area early in 1849), he makes extensive use of dialect words in the Yarmouth chapters. Such terms as *bein*, *dodman*, *mawther*, *clicketen*, *mavish* all appear in Moor's handbook. (Another word, *awize*, is something of a curiosity: it is given thus by Moor but was written *arrize* in Dickens's manuscript. He detected and corrected the error at the proof stage, but the correction was overlooked by the printer and the error has passed into subsequent editions until the present day.) Again, however, dialect is used only for minor characters and for a limited range of effects.

But Dickens's most memorable achievement in dialect writing is by general consent the Cockney which is legion throughout his work. Behind it lies not only a well-established dialect, the features of which had been commented on long before Dickens wrote, but a tradition of literary Cockney in fiction and drama. Behind *Pickwick*, therefore, lies both Dickens's own familiarity with lower-class London speech and his know-ledge of such popular successes of the preceding years as Pierce Egan's *Life in London* and Moncrieff's burlesque ballad-opera *Tom and Jerry* based on Egan's book. The two traditions, the real-life and the literary, obviously share common elements; but just as written Cockney can hardly incor-porate all the features of actual speech, so it will tend to exaggerate the importance of certain elements and to imply that they were more pro-minent in the speech of real Cockneys than was in fact the case. *Pickwick* played an important part in perpetuating a convention of literary Cockney which, as the century progressed, became more and more remote from actual speech. Shaw points out, in an afterword to *Captain Brassbound's*

Conversion, that the Sam Weller dialect was almost extinct when he came to London in 1876, though writers were still reproducing it faithfully. What Shaw takes for granted, but what may reasonably be questioned, is the existence *at any time* of a living dialect corresponding to that of Dickens's novel. A case in point is the celebrated v/w confusion, which certainly existed, in life and literature, before Dickens wrote, but which gained a new popularity in the speech of Sam Weller: there seems to be no evidence that this ever loomed as large in life as in the pages of *Pickwick*, and it has certainly disappeared from present-day Cockney.

But Dickens's primary concern was not, of course, the delineation of living speech. To create a Cockney idiom that would be readily identifiable, adaptable for a variety of characters, entertaining in itself, yet presenting no problems of comprehension in novels intended for a mass readership – this was the problem he set himself to solve. What we do not find in the speech of Sam Weller and his successors (for Dickens was still using Cockney speech in his last novels) is either striking departures from normal syntax, or the extensive use of dialect words, since either might impede easy comprehension. Instead, Dickens isolates and emphasizes certain features of pronunciation, indicates them orthographically often enough to signal the presence of the dialect, but makes no attempt at a complete or consistent rendering. The reader who cares to read the text aloud, or to 'hear' it in his mind as he reads silently, will find enough phonological information thus provided to produce a distinctive effect, if not a completely convincing Cockney; but the signals never cluster so densely as to create the kind of obstacles to rapid reading encountered in Shaw's dialogue, or in some other late-nineteenth-century representations of Cockney:

> Ahrs is a Free Tride nition. It gows agin us as Hinglishmen to see these bloomin furriners settin up their Castoms Ahses and spheres o hinfluence and sich lawk hall owver Arfricar. Daownt Harfricar belong as much to huz as to them? thets wot we say.
>
> [*Captain Brassbound's Conversion*, Act 1]
>
> It wuz afore mah tahm, bet I dess-sy you reckerlec' we'en the 'Owben Viadeck wuz owpin'd? In the middle uv the Viadeck, yer 'now, there's steps a-leadin' daown inter Ferrind'n Rowd enderneath. W'en you've bin a-walkin' in Ferrind'n Rowd, 'ev y'ivver trahd a-kemmin' ep them there steps? The mowst pezzlin' steps in Lendin' I calls 'em. . . .
>
> [Andrew Tuer, *Thenks Awf'lly*, 1890]

In the first scene in which Sam Weller appears (Ch 10) some sixty deviant spellings may be noted, falling into several categories. Among the commonest are the substitution of *-in'* for *-ing*, the omission of certain unaccented syllables (*reg'lar, b'longs*) and of *t* or *d* after certain consonants (*mas'rs, gen'lm'n*), and vowel-changes in such well-established uneducated pronunciations as *babby* and *biled*. Substitution of *v* for *w* is much commoner than the reverse. Sam's subsequent appearances repeat but hardly develop or add to these features: he is like a successful comedian whose audiences prefer the familiar gambits to any novelty. There is a fair sprinkling of inconsistencies: *wery* and *werry*, *wos* and *vas*, *vy* and *vhite* all appear in Chapter 10. Such minor blemishes are hardly likely to trouble the reader; their interest lies in the light they throw on Dickens's frankly selective and at times casual approach to the rendering of dialect.

Sam Weller's linguistic kin are numerous, and the most famous of them, Mrs Gamp in *Martin Chuzzlewit* (1844), shares many of the features of his speech. Her outstanding innovation is the *g* which, orthographically, so often replaces *s* or *z* or, more rarely, *t*, or which simply intrudes, as in *deniged* (denied). There seems to be no firm evidence that this ever existed to a significant extent in the speech of any living Cockney, though there is a literary precedent in Mistress Quickly's *pulsidge* (pulses) (II *Henry* IV, 2, 4). Dickens evidently seized on a minor, or even imaginary, feature of the dialect and, grasping its possibilities for comedy and character-individuation, proceeded to make it one of the identifying features of Mrs Gamp's speech. It perhaps suggests, appropriately, the thickened speech of a confirmed alcoholic. But the important point is that, for Dickens, the comic end justifies the linguistic means: his art is not primarily a realistic one, and in spite of his popular reputation as a historian of London life and manners we must not expect to find in his novels a conscientious representation of observed speech-habits.[8]

Ten years later, *Hard Times* is interesting in a quite different way. Dickens here put a regional dialect to a very different use in the wholly serious, even tragic figure of the factory-hand Stephen Blackpool, whose name indicates his Lancashire origins. Stephen's dialect, like that of Jeanie Deans, is a guarantee of his integrity – the prosperous and hypocritical Bounderby, who comes 'of humble parents' and prides himself upon being a self-made man, shows almost no trace of dialect – but it is also the badge of a downtrodden class. Dickens began to write *Hard Times* early in 1854, visiting Preston at the same period in search of material. A byproduct of the Preston visit was a *Household Words* article 'On Strikes', which contains evidence that his ears had been sensitive to the idiom and pronunciation, as well as to the content, of the Lancashire factory-workers' speech, for he reproduces in that article a speech by a Preston weaver which includes many of the forms which recur in the novel. Stephen's speech was created, then, with vivid impressions of the dialect of the Preston area fresh in the novelist's mind, though his knowledge of it was certainly limited.

Three features of its presentation are especially noteworthy. First, considerable use is made of variant spellings, but the number of actual dialect words used is small. (A possible origin for some of them will be suggested shortly.) Examples of standard words differently spelt include *agen, awlus, chilt, coom, fok, owd; dree, fewtrils* and *hottering* are among the specifically local words. Secondly, the evidence of the manuscript, the corrected proofs and the revisions to which various editions of the novel were subjected seems to indicate that Dickens felt a good deal of uncertainty about the extent to which non-standard spellings should be used. The manuscript *nightb't*, for instance, is changed to *nighbut* at the proof stage; at one point, *yoong* is altered to *young*, though elsewhere the change takes place in the opposite direction; *fok* becomes *folk*, and later reverts to the original reading; *I am come* is first replaced by *I'm come*, then by the more strongly dialectal *I ha' coom*, which is in turn abandoned in favour of *I ha' come*, even though *coom* appears elsewhere.[9] One has the sense of Dickens somewhat anxiously steering a course that will provide adequate indications of dialect speech without running aground on the shoals of obscurity. Thirdly, there is in different parts of the text much variation in the extent to which regional speech is indicated. Consider, for example, the following:

> "I've tried a long time, and 'taint got better. But thou'rt right; 'tmight mak folk talk, even of thee. Thou hast been that to me, Rachael, through so many year: thou hast done me so much good, and heartened of me in that cheering way, that thy word is a law to me. Ah, lass, and a bright good law! Better than some real ones." (Ch 10)

Indications of dialect become noticeably less frequent in the latter half of the passage quoted. The reader has been given sufficient information to suggest the general lines of Stephen's speech, and at normal reading speed the incompleteness is not disconcerting. A similar variation exists between one scene and another: the speech of Chapter 11 is much more heavily marked than that of the preceding chapter. Although this might seem to be the reverse of what is natural on a character's second appearance, the explanation is probably dramatic rather than linguistic: in the scene with Bounderby (Ch 11) Stephen's whole situation, in which his speech is a

major factor, is contrasted with that of his interlocutor. The most frequent reminders of dialect occur at the beginning of the chapter, which
was also the opening of one of the weekly parts as originally published:
apparently Dickens felt the need to recall to the reader's mind an idiom
established earlier, and, having done so, felt that the pressure could be
eased without perceptible ill-effects.

In *Hard Times*, then, Dickens uses for dramatic purposes a dialect of
which his own first-hand knowledge was limited, and which he evidently
feels some uncertainty over reproducing fully and accurately. Not that
accuracy is a prime consideration, since completeness and consistency both
give way at times to the demands of intelligibility. An instructive comparison may be made with another novel written at precisely the same
time and using a similar dialect for a character bearing some resemblance
to Stephen Blackpool, by a writer bringing to the task a much fuller
knowledge than Dickens ever possessed. Like *Hard Times*, Mrs Gaskell's
North and South (1855) was written for serial publication in *Household
Words*, where its publication began only three weeks after the conclusion
of Dickens's novel. Mrs Gaskell had, however, begun her novel in 1853, so
that she is not likely to have been influenced by Dickens's handling of
dialect; indeed, she had nothing to learn from him, whereas he may well
have been influenced by the dialect writing in her earlier novels, which he
is known to have admired. Her use of dialect drew on the continuous
experience of many years. Not only had she lived for more than twenty
years in Manchester, but her husband had a scholarly interest in dialecto-
logy and had written two lectures on the Lancashire dialect which were
subsequently reprinted in the fifth edition of *Mary Barton* (1854). Dickens
read the lectures 'with uncommon pleasure', as he told Mrs Gaskell in a
letter dated 16 June 1854, adding that they 'tell me so much that is interesting'. It may be more than coincidence that some of the words used by
Stephen Blackpool (*dree* and *een* among them) are listed and discussed by
Gaskell in his lectures.

Literary interest in the Lancashire dialect was not new in the 1840s
when Mrs Gaskell began her career as a novelist. Just as *Pickwick* inherits a
long tradition of Cockney writing, her novels have behind them more
than a hundred years of dialect literature, of which the most celebrated
example was *A View of the Lancashire Dialect* (1746) by 'Tim Bobbin'
(John Collier). This was enormously popular (by the end of the nineteenth century it had run into over sixty editions) but was only one of
countless similar works. To glance at the regional list in the sixth volume
of Joseph Wright's *English Dialect Dictionary* is to receive a startling im-

pression of the abundance of material produced in this field by Mrs Gaskell's Lancashire contemporaries: among many others, Edwin Waugh is represented by thirty-four titles, Benjamin Brierley by twenty-one and James T. Staton by twenty. The titles themselves suggest a predominantly humorous and domestic content, and though Mrs Gaskell may have learned something from these books about dialect, her distinctive achievement was to use it not as a mere source of comedy or curiosity, but for dramatic purposes in contexts which exploited the contrast with standard forms of speech.

Nicholas Higgins in *North and South* is a factory-hand who comes 'fro' Burnley-ways, and forty mile to th' North'. This both places Higgins as a Lancastrian and sets the industrial scenes of the novel in the area south of Manchester, not far from either the city where the novelist spent most of her adult life, or from Knutsford in Cheshire where she spent her childhood. Higgins's speech, and that of his daughter Bessy, use a fairly large number of dialect words and expressions, as well as non-standard grammatical forms and very frequent indications of pronunciation. The dialect words include *nesh* and several others discussed in William Gaskell's lectures, and the general authenticity of the vocabulary is confirmed by comparison with a near-contemporary compilation, J. H. Nodal and G. Milner's *Glossary of the Lancashire Dialect* (1875), which includes *clem, deaved, gradely, welly* and others in the senses given them by Mrs Gaskell. It is true that the dialect in *North and South* is still rendered mainly by lexical rather than grammatical features: there is little syntactical difference between the speech of Higgins and that of the characters speaking standard English. (This emphasis also applies to Mr Gaskell's lectures, where the approach is largely philological, and is perhaps typical of the linguistic bias of the period.) But Mrs Gaskell's is still dialogue which benefits from her deep knowledge of the dialect as living speech: compared to Dickens, she employs the dialect more extensively, to convey a wider variety of moods, and Higgins emerges as a more convincing figure than Blackpool. The two novelists bring to the solution of the problem very different backgrounds, and in this instance the lesser writer achieves the greater success: not even Dickens can make a few days in Preston an effective substitute for a long and affectionate awareness of a dialect as the expression of a way of life.

A few years earlier, another northern dialect had been used, with an unusually bold attempt at fidelity, by Emily Brontë. In the first edition of *Wuthering Heights* (1847) the dialect speech of the old Yorkshire servant Joseph is of exceptional vividness and, for many readers, considerable difficulty. His speech seems not to belong to any single West Riding dialect, but to constitute an amalgam of northern elements, with the intrusion of a possible Irish influence in such words as *clane* and *dacent* (Patrick Brontë, we recall, was brought up in Ireland). There are, however, no disconcerting intrusions of words or forms alien to northern dialects, and a substantial effort has been made to suggest the sound-quality of broad Yorkshire speech through spelling variants. What makes the example a particularly interesting one is the subsequent fate of these portions of the dialogue. When Charlotte Brontë, after her sister's death, set about preparing the second edition of the novel (published in 1850), she felt that the virtues of authenticity were not sufficient to outweigh the obstacles to understanding, and wrote to her publisher that

> It seems to me advisable to modify the orthography of the old servant Joseph's speeches; for though as it stands it exactly renders the Yorkshire dialect to a Yorkshire ear, yet I am sure Southerns must find it unintelligible; and thus one of the most graphic characters in the book is lost on them.[10]

Charlotte made this graphic character more readily accessible to the reader by toning down precisely that quality which contributes most to his rough vigour. Some brief quotations from the two versions will indicate the extent of her revision:

> "Noa!" said Joseph ... "Noa! that manes nowt – Hathecliff maks noa 'cahnt uh t'mother, nur yah norther – bud he'll hev his lad; und Aw mun tak him – soa nah yah knaw!" (Ch 19, 1847)
>
> "Noa!" said Joseph ... "Noa! that means naught. Hathecliff maks noa 'count o' t'mother, nor ye norther; but he'll hev his lad; und I mun tak him – soa now ye knaw!" (1850)
>
> "Und hah isn't that nowt comed in frough th' field, be this time? What is he abaht? girt eedle seeght!" demanded the old man, looking round for Heathcliff. (Ch 9, 1847)
>
> "And how isn't that nowt comed in fro' th' field, be this time? What is he about? girt idle seeght!" demanded the old man, looking round for Heathcliff. (1850)

One's surprise at the extent of the revision – there are nine changes in less than thirty words in the short speech from Chapter 19 – is tempered by the reflection that it might have gone even further: that 'girt idle seeght', for instance, may present almost as much difficulty to the reader innocent of the dialect as 'girt eedle seeght'. On the other hand, the replacement of such frequently occurring words as the personal pronouns *Aw* and *yah* by *I* and *ye* makes a significant contribution to easy reading. But it is clear that the gain in intelligibility has only been achieved at the expense of a loss in phonetic precision, and that the Joseph who says *nowt* and *abaht* rather than *naught* and *about* is both more of a Yorkshireman and likely to strike the reader as a more grotesque and uncouth figure. We are likely to agree with most modern editors, therefore, in wishing to discount Charlotte's improvements and to read the novel in the form in which Emily wrote it, though the problem is complicated by the loss of the manuscript and the misprints which seriously mar the first edition. *Wuthering Heights* is interesting both for the thoroughness with which Emily Brontë sought to represent Yorkshire speech, and for the concessions to the average novel-reader made by her sister's revision. Joseph remains, of course, a minor character: one could hardly imagine him charged with the narration of any part of the story. Even Emily seems to have been aware that small helpings of dialect are likely to satisfy the keenest appetite, and it is revealing that Ellen Dean, to whom the majority of the narrative is entrusted, is a very superior kind of servant, and indeed a well-spoken woman with some acquaintance with books and little sign in her speech of her regional origins.

Hardy's dialogue, like Scott's, exhibits a wide variation of quality between the stilted and at times preposterous language of his middle-class characters, and the entirely different diction and rhythms of his rustics. The former too often resembles Hardy's narrative style, itself frequently ponderous and turgid, but the latter breaks with the nineteenth-century traditions of written prose and has a real relationship to spontaneous speech. The worst of his dialogue can be seen in a minor novel such as *A Laodicean* (1881), which offers a bumper crop of absurdities. De Stancy's ' "I have unconsciously adopted Radical notions to obliterate disappointed hereditary instincts" ' will serve as a sample. Even the major novels suffer from lapses of this kind, where Hardy seems to have lost all awareness of living speech. Such dialogue is literary in the sense that it belongs exclusively to the written medium: like much of Scott's, it cannot have been *heard* by the writer, and fails to suggest the spoken language to the reader. No doubt the inhibiting effects of Victorian fictional conventions, and especially his awareness of the requirements and prohibitions of the magazine editors, helped to make such blemishes possible, especially when Hardy is presenting the language of lovers. The natural accents of passion would hardly have found a place in the pages of the *Cornhill*. (Would any editor have touched *Jane Eyre* or *Wuthering Heights*?) His rustic speech has also been criticized as literary in a different sense: in *Under the Green-wood Tree* (1872), for instance, the influence of Shakespeare (who also provides the title), and specifically the clowns of *A Midsummer Night's Dream*, is at times apparent, but it is an influence undeniably modified by Hardy's own deep-rooted sense of the idiom and tones of his native district. A passage, typical of many, in which he succeeds in catching the flavour of natural speech is worth looking at with some care:

> "Really, Reuben, 'tis quite a disgrace to see such a man," said Mrs Dewy ... "And the collar of your coat is a shame to behold – so plastered with dirt, or dust, or grease, or something. Why, wherever could you have got it?"
>
> "'Tis my warm nater in summer-time, I suppose. I always did get in such a heat when I bustle about."
>
> "Ay, the Dewys always were such a coarse-skinned family. There's your brother Bob just as bad – as fat as a porpoise – wi' his low, mean, 'How'st do, Ann?' whenever he meets me. I'd 'How'st do' him indeed! If the sun only shines out a minute, there be you all streaming in the face – I never see!"
>
> "If I be hot week-days, I must be hot Sundays."
>
> "If any of the girls should turn after their father 'twill be a bad look-out for 'em, poor things! None of my family was sich vulgar sweaters, not one of 'em. But, Lord-a-mercy, the Dewys! I don't know how ever I cam' into such a family!"
>
> "Your woman's weakness when I asked ye to jine us. That's how it was, I suppose."   [*Under the Greenwood Tree*, Ch 7]

This is admirably expressive of character, and Hardy reproduces language and rhythm with a skill that can only have come from deep familiarity with this kind of speech. Recollecting such passages, it is easy to ascribe its effect to the use of dialect; yet there are, strictly speaking, no dialect words, and the indications of non-standard grammar and pronunciation are not very numerous. What gives this dialogue its distinctive quality is the command of colloquial idiom: such phrases as *a shame to behold, as fat as a porpoise, a bad look-out*, though not the exclusive property of any specific dialect, would be unlikely to occur in literary prose. They belong not to any individual speaker (had Mrs Dewy ever *seen* a porpoise?) but to a common stock of familiar but vivid expressions embodying traditional attitudes and folk-wisdom. Such expressions give dialogue a timeless, almost ritualistic quality: one feels that the same half-serious protests and complaints, retorts and jests, might have been made innumerable times in the same words. Such formulaic repetition is a characteristic of uneducated speech. The sentence-patterns are also responsible for reinforcing the colloquial impression: note the sentence-endings 'or something', 'I never see!', 'I suppose', and the syntax of

"But, Lord-a-mercy, the Dewys!"

"Your woman's weakness when I asked ye to jine us."

These are not sentences as normally defined for written prose, but they are typical of spontaneous speech. In context, the easy naturalness of this dialogue is all the more striking by contrast with the unusually stilted style of the narrative, a style as remote from spontaneous speech in its vocabulary and syntax as could well be imagined. Its vocabulary shows a preference for the uncommon to the familiar word: surroundings become 'precincts' and a conversation a 'discourse'. No doubt Hardy's intention was to lend dignity to his more formal style, but a side-effect is that the homely directness of the dialogue is like a breath of fresh air. Similarly, the narrative syntax leans towards the elaborate, with accumulated subordinate clauses, and the same effect of contrast obtains.

Hardy's own comments on the presentation of rustic speech insist that accuracy must where necessary yield to the requirements of the work of fiction as a whole:

If a writer attempts to exhibit on paper the precise accents of a rustic speaker he disturbs the proper balance of a true representation by unduly insisting upon the grotesque element; thus directing attention to a point of inferior interest, and diverting it from the speaker's meaning . . .[11]

In other words, striving after close fidelity to life is apt to defeat its own ends: 'the proper balance of a true representation' is to be achieved by selection and modification, by a necessary compromise between suggesting 'the grotesque element' and preventing it from becoming so excessive as to interfere with more important purposes. (One might note in passing that Hardy fails to take into account the impossibility of exhibiting anyone's 'precise accents' in a work of fiction.) A similar point is made in the preface to *The Mayor of Casterbridge*: defending 'the Scotch language of Mr Farfrae', Hardy insists that 'no attempt is made herein to reproduce his entire pronunciation phonetically, any more than that of the Wessex speakers'; at the same time, his concern for regional authenticity is suggested by his enlisting the aid of a 'professor of the tongue in question' (identified as Sir George Douglas) to correct the passages in question for the 1895 edition.

Hardy thus reaches the conclusion that, consciously or otherwise, seems to have been reached by most novelists who have made use of regional dialects. His reluctance to go further is hardly a cause for reproach; as it was, his dialogue was found unreasonably obscure by contemporary reviewers. In an article dated 8 October 1881, the *Spectator* referred to 'Mr Thomas Hardy, whose thorough knowledge of the dialectical peculiarities of certain districts has tempted him to write whole conversations which are, to the ordinary reader, nothing but a series of linguistic puzzles'. It is difficult to guess which 'whole conversations' the writer was thinking of, and one must conclude that modern readers are more practised in reading non-standard dialogue than their Victorian counterparts, perhaps because modern communications have made them more familiar with varieties of speech in everyday life. How far the dialect speech of the Wessex novels was from being a record of actual rustic language can be seen by comparing it with samples of Dorset conversation noted during the same period by Hardy's friend, the poet William Barnes. The following is his record of the reply he received from a countryman who had been questioned about his new waggon: since Barnes is concerned primarily with conveying an accurate notion of the dialect, and not with the larger purposes of fiction, we may probably take it that his rendering is a reliable one:

> Why, the vust thing I do vine fate wi' is the drats; tha be too crooked; and the tug-irons be a-put in mwore than dree inches too vur back. An' jis' look here, where the rudge-tie and breechen rings be: why, nar a carter in the wordle can't put a hoss into en. I don't call the head and täil a-put out 'o han' well. They be a-painted noo-how. Why 'e woon't bear hafe a luoad; tha've a-meäde en o' green stuff a-shook all to pieces. The vust time 'e 's a-haled out in the zun, e'll come all abrode. The strongest thing I do zee about en is the mainpin; and he is too big by hafe.[12]

Though set down without benefit of tape-recorder, Barnes's example is enough to underline the compromise that Hardy's dialogue represents. Even allowing for the subject-matter of Barnes's informant, which naturally encouraged the use of technical terms unfamiliar to the layman, it is obvious that no novel could support dialogue written in this way. Faithfulness to life, so often invoked in praise of dialogue, would be a very doubtful virtue if it were ever practised.

The drama in many of Hardy's novels comes from the intrusion of middle-class characters into the lives of the humble, and their speech is one of the most prominent devices for denoting these inhabitants of two contrasted worlds. Some of the most interesting characters, furthermore, represent in themselves the conflict between two ways of life, each with its appropriate speech habits. Tess is perhaps the first bilingual heroine in English fiction, and the first tragic figure whose troubles spring partly from the spread of education. Whereas her mother speaks 'the dialect', Tess, who has attended the National School 'under a London-trained mistress', speaks dialect at home and 'ordinary English' beyond it. Similar bilingualism is found in the work of D. H. Lawrence, where characters are shown deliberately switching from dialect to standard English and back again, or from a stronger to a weaker form of the dialect, according to the tone of a particular scene and the relationships involved. These variations are unlike the inconsistencies noted in earlier writers, which were dictated by technique, since they correspond to an actual variation which is to be supposed dramatically to be taking place in the speech of the character.   There can be no doubt that Lawrence's background made him, like Dickens, sensitive to the linguistic tokens of social mobility. As a boy, we are told, 'he had an intimate knowledge of the local dialect which is a mixture of border Nottinghamshire and Derbyshire'; but the following comments by his younger sister Ada on their mother's attitude to speech suggest that his use of dialect was not uninhibited:

> Some people were ill-natured enough to say that she 'put it on' when she spoke, for her English was good and her accent so different from that of the folk round about. Try as she might, she could never speak the local dialect, and we children were careful about it when we were with her, even though we let fling among our friends.[13]

This tallies closely with the Morel family in *Sons and Lovers* (1913), where the father's speech is broadly dialectal, whereas Mrs Morel uses few local words and altogether eschews the *thou* and *thee* forms favoured by her husband. Nor does her speech suggest non-standard pronunciation, as his constantly does. Her linguistic righteousness extends to her children— though with some exceptions, for in moments of intimacy Paul reverts to dialect. In the same way, Mellors in *Lady Chatterley's Lover* (1928) uses dialect to express tenderness – switching to it somewhat ostentatiously from the standard English he at other times employs. The effect is thus the opposite from that created by Stephen Blackpool's confrontation with Bounderby in *Hard Times*: Mellors's dialect implies not unavoidable social disadvantage but a natural warmth and emotional closeness in which status is temporarily forgotten. Lawrence uses dialect, that is, not primarily for local colour and social contrast, but to distinguish the language of intimacy from that of more formal or commonplace relationships. In this respect he is anticipated by George Eliot, who writes of Adam Bede that 'whenever he wished to be especially kind to his mother, he fell into his strongest native accent and dialect, with which at other times his speech was less deeply tinged'   [*Adam Bede*, Ch 4].

At different times, therefore, dialect can serve opposite purposes – to bring characters closer together by signalling an increase in emotional pressure, since dialect is associated with childhood or with one's most intimate relationships and informal moods; or to draw them apart, by emphasizing a social gulf or acting as an unpleasant reminder of humble origins. This last function is illustrated by a passage in Hardy's *The Mayor of Casterbridge* (1886, Ch 20), when Elizabeth remarks to her father:

> ... wishing to show him something, "If you'll bide where you be a minute, father, I'll get it."
>
> "'Bide where you be,'" he echoed sharply. "Good God, are you only fit to carry wash to a pig-trough, that ye use such words as those?"
>
> She reddened with shame and sadness.
>
> "I meant 'Stay where you are,' father," she said, in a low, humble voice. "I ought to have been more careful."

The incident contributes to the increasingly strained relationship between them; henceforth, we learn, the girl watches her linguistic behaviour more carefully, remembering to say 'humble bees' rather than 'dumbledores', and to speak of having 'suffered from indigestion' rather than of being 'hag-rid'. Behind the passage we may sense Hardy's wry attitude towards the impoverishment of familiar discourse involved in observing the canons of propriety. There is perhaps a specific irony in Henchard's own switch from *you* to the non-standard *ye* under the stress of feeling as he rebukes Elizabeth.

With Lawrence's gamekeeper, dialect has travelled a long way from the earlier fictional tradition of Fielding, Smollett and the young Dickens. From being almost exclusively a badge of the ignorant, the foolish, the crude or the socially inferior, it has become a 'little language' reserved for moments of special significance: the bilingual Mellors, is, linguistically as well as sexually, a better man than his employer, who is imprisoned in the cold formality of standard speech as he is in his wheelchair. Since Lawrence wrote, many factors have helped to modify the novel-reader's attitude towards dialect. Sound broadcasting has made regional speech more familiar than ever before; a meritocratic society has permitted regional pronunciations, if not dialect in the full sense, to invade such citadels as the BBC and the senior common rooms of universities; increased mobility and educational opportunity have had the effect of making many people bilingual within English, reserving regional speech, like Tess, for their homes and using standard forms in their work or in society at large; yet, alongside all this, the music-hall tradition of speech variants as comic *per se* is not entirely dead. The present-day reader is, thanks to radio, cinema and television, incomparably better informed concerning regional speech than his eighteenth- and nineteenth-century ancestors. He is likely to recognize the accents, and understand the vocabulary, of Brooklyn or Brisbane more readily than many earlier readers probably coped with the speech of Somerset or Scotland. All of which must make itself felt in terms of imaginative response to the written word, and re-creation of what it so inadequately stands for. At the same time, our reading, unlike that of the Victorians, is mainly silent reading; and the loss, even if it cannot be estimated with accuracy, must be appreciable, affecting much more than questions of dialect.

Any shift in attitude towards regional speech in life is likely to modify our response when we meet it in literature and, sooner or later, to affect the practice of writers. It will be interesting to see whether the more tolerant attitude that has developed in recent years will bring to an end the long tradition of comic dialect. Certainly such post-war novelists as Stan Barstow, Alan Sillitoe and David Storey use various forms of regional speech for serious purposes, though a more traditional novelist like Angus Wilson tends to equate non-standard speech with comic or grotesque effects. Meanwhile, outside Britain, a new kind of interest is to be found in the overseas varieties of English which have established themselves, or are in the process of doing so, and in which a literature is beginning to arise. Our response to the dialogue of V. S. Naipaul or Amos Tutuola may give us some notion of how the speech of Lancashire or Somerset struck earlier generations.

In a society sensitive to departures from the standard language, dialect has traditionally provided a ready means whereby eccentricity, or at least individuality, can be signalled. More seriously, it can bear a relationship to character, suggesting (for instance) unaffected simplicity or rugged independence in contrast to the uniformity and artificiality represented by the standard language. Even more profoundly, a dialect may express the way of life of its users, and, however imperfectly the novelist may present it, some sense of this may come across to the reader. Since reading is a joint enterprise, the knowledge and assumptions of the reader will be almost as important as the skill and purpose of the writer. At the simplest level, he may respond by recognizing that dialect is something other than standard speech; he may go a little further, and associate the dialect (possibly with the writer's help) with a specific region, and with that region's history and traditions; or, on the basis of his own experience, he may make a close identification of the written dialect with particular qualities of the spoken language. Not every reader will make this full response, nor is it likely that every novelist expects it.

The language of non-native users of English is perhaps not strictly a dialect, but it may be conveniently dealt with at this point, together with the curious but widespread convention of indicating the use of a foreign language by means of a variety of English. Under the general heading of 'foreign speech', therefore, two quite different categories must be distinguished: one is 'broken English', English speech more or less strongly marked with evidence of various kinds that the speaker is not using his mother-tongue; the other is idiosyncratic dialogue written in English but to be taken as representing a foreign tongue. The two kinds represent different degrees of convention and stand at different distances from a hypothetical norm of 'realistic' speech. The first may include elements observed in actuality – features commonly found when English is spoken less than perfectly by (say) a Frenchman. Since these imperfections may be partly the result of 'interference' by the speaker's mother tongue, the particular features will vary according to whether he is a Frenchman, a Russian, or a Chinese. The second kind is entirely a matter of convention, comparable to such frankly non-realistic forms as the blank-verse soliloquy.

Broken English offers an easily exploited source of comedy:

"I demand of you a thousand pardons, monsieur. I am without defence. For some months now I cultivate the marrows. This morning suddenly I enrage myself with these marrows. I send them to promenade themselves – alas ! not only mentally but physically. I seize the biggest. I hurl him over the wall. Monsieur, I am ashamed. I prostrate myself."   [Agatha Christie, *The Murder of Roger Ackroyd*, 1926]

Even the reader ignorant of French can respond to the picturesque inaccuracy of Poirot's idiom. Its main device is the literal translation of a French word or phrase into an English one, similar in sound and form, but not quite equivalent in meaning (*demand, enrage myself, promenade themselves*), with a discreet topping of widely-known French terms (here represented by *monsieur*). The oddity of such speech is soon exhausted, and its capacity for expressing character or mood very limited. A more dramatic instance occurs in Dickens's *Bleak House*. The French lady's-maid Hortense was probably based on a real-life prototype, the murderess Maria Manning, born Marie de Roux, who was also a lady's-maid before her marriage. (Dickens witnessed her execution in 1849, and had no doubt read newspaper accounts of her appearance in court, described in Griffiths's *Chronicles of Newgate*: 'speaking with a foreign accent, [she] addressed the court with great fluency and vehemence'.) Hortense uses inexact equivalents for French words (*droll* for *amusing*, *domestic* for *servant*) and expressions (*since five years*, *on the moment*), and the manuscript of the novel shows Dickens's concern to emphasize this element in her speech: he cancelled *fondled*, for example, in favour of the Romance equivalent *caressed*. He also indicates features of pronunciation and stress (*des-pise, det-est, en-r-r-r-raged*) as well as showing how her command of lexis and morphology deteriorates as her passion rises: '"You have attrapped me – catched me –"'.

When a foreign language is being spoken, the writer has the choice of indicating this by authorial statement or of incorporating appropriate signals within the dialogue itself. Dickens often resorts unblushingly to the former, as in the opening chapter of *Little Dorrit*:

"I have brought your bread, Signor John Baptist," said he (they all spoke in French, but the little man was an Italian).

and in the confrontation of Miss Pross and Madame Defarge in *A Tale of Two Cities* (III, 14):

Each spoke in her own language; neither understood the other's words; both were very watchful, and intent to deduce from look and manner, what the unintelligible words meant.

In *Dombey and Son* (Ch 54) a French servant brings supper to Edith at a Dijon inn:

She started up, and cried, "Who's that?" The answer was in French . . .

But when the servant's dialogue is given, it is, of course, in English, though marked by the use of French expressions (*en route*) and by words and expressions recalling French usage – a very similar variety, in fact, to that used for Hortense's broken English.

A different approach from that of Dickens is found in a novel of the same period, Charlotte Brontë's *Villette*, set largely in Belgium. When the heroine Lucy Snowe arrives at Madame Beck's school, she confesses her ignorance of spoken French, and her isolation – linguistic as well as emotional – is an important element in her situation. Madame Beck's first words to her are in broken English ("'You ayre Engliss?'"), but in the ensuing dialogue direct speech is at any rate temporarily shelved:

> She proceeded to work away volubly in her own tongue. I answered in mine. . . . We made together an awful clamour. . . . (Ch 7)

There follows a second stage in which direct speech is used, the Belgian woman speaking French, given as such in the novel, and Lucy speaking English. Finally, there is a swift transition to a third stage in which the French-speaking characters are given dialogue in English to represent their French conversation, though it is a variety of English which includes an admixture of French words and phrases. By this time, the following dialogue can be conducted in Lucy's presence without apparent incongruity:

> "She speaks French?"
> "Not a word."
> "She understands it?"
> "No."
> "One may then speak plainly in her presence?"
> "Doubtless."

Charlotte Brontë has reached the same point as Dickens, where English dialogue can be understood to represent foreign speech, but she has taken much longer to do so: whereas he plunges into the full use of the convention, she adopts it only after a transitional passage which seems to have the purpose of preparing the ground for the necessary illusion. No doubt the difference corresponds to a difference in the degree of realism aimed at, but there is also a contrast in the demands made on the reader's acquaintance with a foreign language (as well as, one may add, the writer's). In Hemingway's *For Whom the Bell Tolls* (1940) the English-speaking hero is to be taken as using Spanish extensively, and most of the other characters are Spanish. Like Dickens's French dialogue, Hemingway's Spanish is partly written in a variety of English strongly suggesting Spanish idiom:

> "How do they call thee?"
> "That . . . is much horse."
> "He spoke in a very rare manner."

Other examples include the frequent use of *clearly* (corresponding to *claro*) where *of course* would be more natural in English conversation, and such usages as *assassinate* (*asesinar*) for *murder*. This has the double effect of producing a sense of foreignness and of ceremonious dignity. But Hemingway also uses Spanish words and sentences freely, sometimes supplying an English equivalent before or after the Spanish, and sometimes relying on the context to make the meaning clear:

"*Nada*," said Anselmo. "Nothing."
"*Me voy*," the gipsy said. "I go."
"Thick head. *Tonto*."
"The *mujer* of Pablo . . ."

A final, more exotic example may be given from *Things Fall Apart* (1958) by the Nigerian novelist Chinua Achebe, who uses a stylized variety of English, with a few untranslatable non-English words, to convey the sense of an African vernacular. Such speech is often formal, making frequent use of metaphorical and proverbial language: '"my children do not resemble me"', complains Okonkwo at one point, adding quite unself-consciously, '"Where are the young suckers that will grow when the old banana tree dies?"' There is also some explicit comment on the speech situation, as when the white missionary speaks through an Ibo interpreter of a different tribe: the latter's dialect

was different and harsh to the ears of Mbanta. Many people laughed at his dialect and the way he used words strangely. Instead of saying "myself" he always said "my buttocks".

Idiosyncratic speech here is much more than an interesting curiosity: it stresses the alien nature of the culture and modes of thinking and feeling to which it gives expression. In a later novel, *Man of the People* (1966), Achebe shows the mixed linguistic situation in a single family: of the Nangas, the father speaks alternately English and Pidgin, the mother her African vernacular 'with the odd English word thrown in now and then', and the children, who have been taught by Europeans at expensive private schools, perfect British English. In a multilingual society the contrast of languages or dialects between different speakers, or the choice of one or other form at a given moment, may carry its own dramatic significance.

In discussing regional dialects in the novel, our examples have included the speech of the Scots peasantry and that of the factory-workers of Lancashire. These and other examples show that regional and social dialects cannot be treated as entirely independent phenomena. Stephen

Blackpool's speech marks him as both an inhabitant of a northern industrial town and a man who, by birth and education, belongs to the working class. And whilst the use of most regional dialects and accents has
traditionally been taken as a sign of humble status (though the tradition
shows signs of weakening), certain features of vocabulary, grammar and
pronunciation are widely regarded as common in uneducated speech,
regardless of regional origins. To talk of 'cowcumber' or 'sparrow-grass',
to say 'I were' at the wrong time or 'we was' at any time, to leave certain words unaspirated or to intrude needless aspirates – such usages are
tokens of social inferiority, or at least this is what novelists and dramatists
find it convenient to assume. Since society is a more amorphous and
shifting entity than geography, however, social dialects are less satis-
factorily defined than regional ones. 'Lower class' or 'upper middle class'
are conspicuously vaguer terms than 'Dorset' or 'West Riding'. Nevertheless, the phenomenon is important enough in English society and the
English novel to call for discussion. It also seems to be a long-standing one.
When Rosalind claims to be a native of the Forest of Arden (*As You Like
It*, 3, 2), Orlando comments rather suspiciously: '"Your accent is something finer than you could purchase in so removed a dwelling"'. Her
speech obviously betrays her upper-class origins: it is as if Lady Bracknell
had suddenly turned up among Hardy's rustics.

Within different novels, the social range depicted varies considerably,
and social differences in speech may be indicated either broadly, as often
by Dickens and Hardy, or more subtly, as by Jane Austen, or may be
simply ignored. (Ignoring them is not necessarily a token of an author's
lack of interest: as the next chapter will show, in certain situations the
significance of social status as a determinant of speech may be overridden
by other, more urgent demands.) Often an author's use of social distinctions in speech is not merely descriptive but comic or satiric, whether
the target be aristocratic affectation or proletarian absurdity. The tradition of comic dialogue satirizing the speech habits of a given class ante-
dates the rise of the novel. Mistress Quickly is a familiar example of
lower-class speech, whilst the Restoration stage is crowded with male
and female figures uttering a stylized upper-class dialect which no doubt
had its origins in real life. In the eighteenth-century novel, the language of
the ruling class is clearly distinguished from that of the servants, who wear
their colloquial vocabulary and non-standard grammar like a uniform.
(The tradition survives until the twentieth century in the Cockney house-
maids and chauffeurs of much popular entertainment.) Such lower-class
dialects are tolerable only for minor characters, however, and when a

servant becomes a major figure, like Richardson's Pamela, she receives a silent rise in linguistic status. As society changes and the clear distinctions of rank become blurred, speech in the novel becomes a more subtle index of status or, even more revealingly, of aspiration. In the nineteenth-century novel we find speech used to mark the social riser, like Mrs Elton or Guppy, as well as the character who has found or who accepts his position in society. Jane Austen, who makes no use of regional dialects, provides many instances of a highly class-conscious attitude to speech. In this she learned much from Fanny Burney, whose *Evelina* (1778) shows an excellent sense of contemporary speech and presents a wide range of social types. Fanny Burney is particularly sensitive to the slang and vulgarisms of such characters as the Branghtons, who proclaim their essential vulgarity every time they open their mouths. One of her favourite devices is the italicizing of such expressions, presumably to make it clear to the reader that the offending word or phrase is not offered unawares: 'Among other questions, they also asked if I had ever seen *such a thing as an Opera?*' and at a ball Evelina is 'accosted by another, who *begged the favour of hopping a dance* with me'. Some of the colloquial usages must have struck the novel's first readers as possessing an up-to-the-minute quality: Mr Branghton's *take-in*, for example, is the earliest use recorded by the *OED*; and *Evelina* remains a valuable source for late-eighteenth-century familiar speech, subject of course to the reservation that must accompany all literary use of the spoken language.

Behind Jane Austen's depicting of social distinctions through speech lies a generation or more of discussion of the doctrine of correctness. As K. C. Phillipps has pointed out, 'If Lucy Steele had lived a century earlier, her worst solecisms would have passed muster'.[14] An eighteenth-century grammarian, Withers, had advised against the use of familiar expressions:

> *To leave in the Lurch* – and *to swallow contradictions* – are Ideas, which may be elegantly expressed by a thousand Modes of Circumlocution, and to Circumlocution I counsel the Student to have Recourse on all similar Occasions.[15]

The main objection to such phrases was doubtless their association with the humbler classes of society; and the attitude persisted well into the nineteenth century, as many Victorian novels illustrate. Mrs Gibson in Mrs Gaskell's *Wives and Daughters* objects to 'such vulgar expressions' as 'Sunday Best' and 'the apple of his eye'; Mrs Vincy in George Eliot's *Middlemarch* is reproved by her socially ambitious daughter for speaking of 'the pick of' the young men in the town, and later by her son for her amended version of the phrase, 'the most superior young men', both phrases carrying to the socially sensitive ear uncongenial overtones; and Lily Dale in Trollope's *Last Chronicle of Barset* scandalizes her mother by her use of the term *skedaddled*. Dickens's Mrs General (in *Little Dorrit*) is a more overtly satirical caricature of Victorian linguistic class-consciousness: '"Papa is a preferable mode of address . . . Father is rather vulgar, my dear"'. All these examples come from the third quarter of the century.

Socially varied modes of speech also provide contrast and colour in a novel portraying a wide range of characters. Dickens is most readily associated with the rendering of lower-class speech, but he presents aristocratic speech in such figures as Lord Verisopht in *Nicholas Nickleby* and Sir Leicester Dedlock in *Bleak House*. The element of caricature common to both is suggested by their names; but the two examples, fourteen years apart, exemplify respectively a naive and a more mature approach. Verisopht belongs to the type of 'silly ass' aristocrat also found in Restoration comedy and in the novels of P. G. Wodehouse: he speaks 'with broken ejaculations', and the bleating quality of his speech, in such pronunciations as are represented by *deyvle, wa-a-x work, ma-ke*, is given prominence. This is the characteristic labelled 'baa' by A. P. Rossiter, who describes it as 'the mark of that past age when being bored was fashionable: when a sort of idiocy (real or assumed) was the mark of class'.[16] In *Bleak House* idiotic boredom is personified by the nameless 'debilitated cousin', whose brief utterances exhibit an extreme form of slurred and elliptical speech: idleness and parasitism, it seems, have reduced not merely action but even language to a minimum (see example [2e], p 163 below).[17]

Sir Leicester, on the other hand, is both a satiric portrait and a figure capable of real dignity and even pathos. An *Athenaeum* reviewer of 1853 judged him 'a true gentleman', and it is a measure of Dickens's mature skill that Sir Leicester survives the parodic element in his speech which is stressed in the early part of the novel. His most trivial observations are expressed in formal diction and elaborate structure: when he calls on Mr Jarndyce in Chapter 43 his first three utterances are of 90, 85 and 88 words in length. His fondness for abstract nouns and well-worn clichés is symptomatic of his tendency towards general judgments and established opinions.

Turveydrop in the same novel, with Mantalini in *Nicholas Nickleby*, represents a corruption of the aristocratic manner transplanted to a lower class. Turveydrop is an anachronism, the Regency buck surviving into an epoch that has no place for him, his synthetic gallantry made all the more ridiculous and offensive by his years: '"Wooman, lovely Wooman, what a sex you are!"' His mannered speech is accompanied by a stylized use of gesture, and he is constantly seen 'waving his gloves condescendingly', 'kissing his right glove', 'taking a pinch of snuff and gently fluttering his fingers', 'kissing the tips of his left fingers'. This use of gesture is both effective and, apparently, authentic: the anonymous author of *The Habits of Good Society* (c 1860) comments on the passing of 'the old courteous dignity with which the beaux of my younger days behaved', but at the same time admits that 'It often amounted to affectation; it was not natural to be ever bowing low, making set speeches, raising a lady's hands to one's lips, or pressing one's own upon the region of the heart...'[18] Turveydrop obviously had many real-life counterparts.

At the other end of the social scale, Dickens displays throughout his career a ceaseless interest in rendering lower-class speech. From the *Sketches by Boz* onwards, a crowd of figures, widows and pawnbrokers, landladies and mountebanks, speak a language which is the sign of their class. An early example from the *Sketches* shows Dickens not yet using the variant spellings which were to play such a part in his later dialogue, but exploiting a deliberate syntactical confusion to reveal the disorganized thought-processes of the uneducated:

> "I rents a two-pair back, gentlemen, at Mrs Brown's, Number 3, Little King William's Alley, which has lived there this fifteen year, and knows me to be very hard-working and industrious, and when my poor husband was alive, gentlemen, as died in the hospital – "

There was nothing new about the representation of such speech, which is common among Dickens's predecessors in the writing of popular fiction. Bulwer's *Paul Clifford* (1835) can stand as an example: '"Vy, Laus-a-me!"' observes one low-life character in that novel, '"If you ben't knocked o' the head! your pole's as bloody as Murphy's face ven his throat's cut!"' Bulwer finds it necessary to explain 'as bloody as Murphy's face' in a footnote, a practice not resorted to by Dickens. The great achievement of the latter was to use such language not just as picturesque local colour but in the service of widely varied character-creation, always distinctive yet usually presenting no obscurities.

Low-life dialogue like the example quoted often makes use of slang, though slang is not the monopoly of any class. Mayhew, in his accounts of conversations with men and women in the London streets, reports a crossing-sweeper as saying, 'When we are talking together we always talk in a kind of slang',[19] and Jo, the orphan crossing-sweeper in *Bleak House*, uses contemporary slang as one of the ingredients of the uncouth speech which marks him as isolated, linguistically as well as in other ways, from most of the other characters in the novel. One of the most striking passages in the book, dramatizing the gulf between the two nations of rich and poor, occurs when Jo meets Lady Dedlock, who offers him money to show her the way to the graveyard:

> "I'm fly," says Jo. "But fen larks, you know ! Stow hooking it!"
> "What does the horrible creature mean?" . . .
> "Stow cutting away, you know!" says Jo.
> "I don't understand you . . ."

Nor, without footnotes or a dictionary of slang, will the present-day reader, in all probability; for while slang has the advantage of imparting a colloquial flavour to dialogue with great ease, it has the serious disadvantage of dating very rapidly and thereby losing much of its force. As anyone who reads Kipling's *Stalky and Co* will find, the colloquialisms of one generation – particularly those of a specific social or other group, which enjoyed an esoteric appeal even when current – have a peculiarly faded air to the next; dialogue, therefore, which is intended to convey a vigour and freshness of which the standard language is deemed incapable ends up as irredeemably fossilized. In *The Sun Also Rises* (1926), Hemingway satirizes the smart slang of his upper-class English characters:

> What a lot of bilge I could think up at night. What rot – I could hear Brett say it. What rot! When you were with English you got into the habit of using English expressions in your thinking. The English spoken language – the upper classes, anyway – must have fewer words than the Eskimo . . .

With its tendency to fade quickly, and its inherently repetitive and monotonous quality, slang evidently presents special dangers to the serious novelist; for the humorist (*cf* the work of P. G. Wodehouse which dates from the same period as Hemingway's novel), who need not fear if language draws attention to itself by its oddity, the risks are less grave. It is possible that the widespread use of slang and colloquialisms in the contemporary British and American novel, which now strike us as refreshingly and vigorously realistic, may be regarded quite differently by readers of future generations.

Although regional and social dialects have been discussed separately, methodological convenience should not be allowed to obscure the fact that in practice they often operate in conjunction, a character's social class serving to moderate or accentuate local features, and the prevailing social situation at a given moment also exerting an influence on the strength of the dialect. The following two examples of nineteenth-century Scots dialect speech, for example, show some significant differences:

1 The listing was a catching distemper. Before the summer was over, other three of the farming lads went off with the drum, and there was a wailing in the parish, which made me preach a touching discourse. I likened the parish to a widow woman with a small family, sitting in their cottage by the fireside, herself spinning with an eident wheel, ettling her best to get them a bit and a brat, and the poor weans all canty about the hearthstane – the little ones at their playocks, and the elder at their tasks – the callans working with hooks and lines to catch them a meal of fish in the morning – and the lassies working stockings to sell at the next Marymass fair. – And then I likened war to a calamity coming among them – the callans drowned at their fishing – the lassies led to a misdoing – and the feckless wee bairns laid on the bed of sickness, and their poor forlorn mother sitting by herself at the embers of a cauldrife fire; her tow done and no a bodle to buy more; dropping a silent and salt tear for her babies, and thinking of days that war gone. . . .
    They both told me that they had never heard such a good discourse; but I do not think they were great judges of preachings. How indeed could Mr Howard know anything of sound doctrine, being educated, as he told me, at Eton school, a prelatic establishment. Nevertheless, he was a fine lad; and though a little given to frolic and diversion, he had a principle of integrity, that afterwards kythed into much virtue; for during this visit, he took a notion of Effie Malcolm, and the lassie of him, then a sprightly and blooming creature, fair to look upon, and blithe to see.   [Galt, *Annals of the Parish* 1821, Ch 17]

2 "I've been thinkin't owre, a' up an' doon. It's a queer thing far ye begin to luik back owre a' the time bygane. The apos'le speaks o' the life o' man as a 'vawpour that appeareth for a little, and then vainisheth awa' '; an' seerly there cudna be a mair nait'ral resem'lance. Fan we begood the pilget there thegither, wi' three 'tirms, an' a bran' it coo't cam' wi' your providin', the tae side o' the place was ta'en up wi' breem busses an' heather knaps half doon the faul'ies and the tither was feckly a quaakin' bog, growin' little but sprots an' rashes. It luiks like yesterday fan we hed the new hooses biggit, an' the grun an' onner the

bleuch, though that's a gweed therty year syne. I min' as bricht's a
paintet pictur' fat like ilka knablich an' ilka sheugh an' en' rig was."
[W. Alexander, *Johnny Gibb of Gushetneuk*, 1871, Ch 44]

Galt's minister switches from a variety of English only lightly marked
with regional words to a more broadly regional speech, and back again,
the contrast underlining the different nature of his sermon, the 'touching
discourse' preached to those more easily reached through the vernacular,
and his dry comments on it, in the first two sentences and the last paragraph quoted. As an educated man, the minister has the two forms of
speech as his disposal, and uses them on different occasion and for different purposes. Alexander's farmer, on the other hand, a moralist by
inclination rather than profession, is a man of less education and speaks
consistently in an idiolect that is broadly dialectal – perhaps excessively
so for the tastes of some readers.

'Each profession', writes G. L. Brook, 'tends to develop its own linguistic idiosyncrasies, of which its members are usually unconscious'.[20]
This is much more obviously true of some occupations than of others, but
it will be generally agreed that a speaker may be betrayed, even in off-
duty hours, as a schoolmaster or clergyman, actor or salesman. The
lawyer will use a strongly-marked occupational dialect, with distinctive
lexical, grammatical and phonological features, in court, and, to a lesser
extent, in professional consultations, as well as in drafting documents and
conducting correspondence, and some of this may overflow into his more
informal discourse with colleagues and friends – though perhaps hardly
so far as his wife and children, his hairdresser or tobacconist. Where the
spoken word is a less important professional tool than in the examples
cited, and where speech is correspondingly less exposed to professional
influences, occupational aspects may be less apparent, but even the brick-
layer, the refuse-collector and the farm-labourer will show some evidence
of their callings, if only by the existence of a specialized vocabulary.
Whether in real life this has much effect upon their non-professional use
of language – whether, for instance, individual differences attributable to
their various occupations can be detected in the speech of a number of
men discussing politics or the weather – may be open to question. For the
novelist, however, it is often useful to assume that they may.

It has already become clear that two questions are involved. One relates to the use of occupational dialects in professional life, and this is a
well-founded linguistic fact confirmed by everyday observation, every
pursuit boasting at least its own jargon of specialized terms and familiar

terms in specialized senses. (*Register*, for example, means different things
to a teacher, a linguist and a clarinettist.) The other concerns occupational
dialects in private life: largely, it may be, a convention, though a widely-
employed one. The first has enjoyed a long tradition: from Chaucer and
Shakespeare onwards, the speech of many characters has been shown to
be subdued to what they work in. If a writer's own knowledge of a
specialized vocabulary is inadequate, he may take pains to collect authentic
material, as Dickens did for the dialogue of the circus-folk in *Hard Times*.[21]
Or he may fall back upon a conventionalized dialect in which every
sailor cries 'Shiver my timbers!' Literary precedent may also be powerful
and many fictional sailors, for instance, owe a debt to the creations of
Smollett. The use of an occupational dialect in private life gives scope for
comic incongruity; thus, Guppy's proposal to Esther in *Bleak House*
mingles the language of a Victorian valentine with that of legal processes,
and Uncle Toby's hobby-horse in *Tristram Shandy* leads him to speak of
everyday matters in terms of a military campaign.

Finally, as well as the slang which serves to mark social class, there are
various kinds of professional slang or cant, of actors and soldiers, schoolboys and university students, serving to create an exclusive group-sense
and to mystify outsiders in the same way as the back-slang of street-
vendors. Again, Dickens provides an example in the language of pugil-
istic circles:

> The Chicken himself attributed this punishment to his having the
> misfortune to get into chancery early in the proceedings, when he was
> severely fibbed by the Larkey one, and heavily grassed. But it appeared
> from the published records that . . . the Chicken had been tapped, and
> bunged, and had received pepper, and had been made groggy, and had
> come up piping . . . until he had been gone into and finished.
>
> [*Dombey and Son*, Ch 44]

Most of the expressions in this short anthology of prize-fighting terms
may be found in Eric Partridge's invaluable *Dictionary of Slang and Unconventional English* (1961). A more widely-used source of cant, however, is
the language of the criminal classes. Underworld slang was a prominent
feature of the so-called 'Newgate novel' as practised by Bulwer and
Ainsworth, and the tradition persists in *Oliver Twist* (1838), the Clarendon
Edition of which provides a glossary of nearly a hundred items. The
Artful Dodger in particular is given a mode of speech rich in such words
as *beak, flash, green, magpie,* in cant usages; Oliver, on the other hand,
shows an innocence (probably shared by the reader) of this language, and

a phrase like 'fogles and ticklers' (handkerchiefs and watches) is glossed
for his benefit within the dialogue – Dickens's solution to the problem of
using an idiom that undeniably adds colour but, without safeguards, may
puzzle and irritate the reader. The tradition continues throughout the
century in such novels of the London underworld as Arthur Morrison's
A Child of the Jago (1896) and survives in the crime fiction of our own
time.

As many of the foregoing examples have suggested, it is dangerous to
use literary dialogue, in fiction or drama, as a basis for assumptions about
the prevailing features of common speech in earlier periods, even though
this has been a frequent practice of historians of the spoken language. The
nature of the written medium makes it inevitable that there should be
considerable adaptation of the features of actual speech, by omission,
modification and exaggeration, in the process of transposing it into visible
form. Such terms of praise as 'authentic' and 'realistic' are to be understood, therefore, in a strictly relative sense: Emily Brontë's Yorkshire
dialogue in *Wuthering Heights* shows an immensely deeper knowledge
and care than that of Dickens in *Nicholas Nickleby*, but it remains essentially a compromise between the recording of the observed features of
Yorkshire speech and a literary dialect accommodated to what the reader,
and the overall purposes of the novel, could tolerate. It is clear, too, that
such signals as the writer invents or borrows to suggest oral quality are
commonly utilized with a calculated and entirely justified inconsistency,
since for most novelists the primary aim is not linguistic accuracy. Having
said this, however, it can fairly be claimed that local and other varieties
of speech, however partially and imperfectly represented, enormously
widen the range of fictional dialogue, and give a distinctive flavour to
many novels (by no means confined to those traditionally regarded as
'regional') that could not easily be supplied by other means.

Notes

1 G. Tillotson, 'Trollope's Style', in *Mid-Victorian Studies* (with K. Tillotson),
   1965, 56. For a contrary view, see my 'Trollope's Conversational Mode', *English
   Studies in Africa*, 15, 1972, 33–7.
2 On early examples of regional dialects in literature, see H. Kökeritz, 'Shakespeare's Use of Dialect', *Transactions of the Yorkshire Dialect Society*, 51, 1951, 10–25.
3 I owe this example to M. Schlauch, *The English Language in Modern Times*,
   Warsaw, 1959, 163.
4 W. A. Boggs, 'Dialectal Ingenuity in *Humphry Clinker*', *Papers on English Language and Literature*, 1, 1965, 327–37.

5 Quoted by J. M. S. Tompkins, *The Popular Novel in England 1770–1800*, 1932, 188, who notes in the late-eighteenth-century novel occasional instances of dialect writing and even 'sporadic attempts to suggest dialectal pronunciation'. She adds that the West of England dialects are especially prominent, no doubt thanks to the example of Fielding's Squire Western.

6 I. Jack, *English Literature 1815–1832*, Oxford, 1963, 212.

7 This was pointed out by K. J. Fielding in *The Times Literary Supplement* for 30 April 1949, 288.

8 The most exhaustive analysis of Dickens's attempts to suggest qualities of pronunciation through the written word is by S. Gerson, *Sound and Symbol in the Dialogue of the Works of Charles Dickens*, Stockholm, 1967. See also J. Saxe, *Bernard Shaw's Phonetics: A Comparative Study of Cockney Sound-changes*, Copenhagen, 1936.

9 See the textual notes in *Hard Times*, ed G. Ford and S. Monod, New York, 1966.

10 *The Brontës: Their Lives, Friendships and Correspondence*, ed Wise and Symington, Oxford, 1932, III, 165. *Cf* also C. Dean, 'Joseph's Speech in *Wuthering Heights*', *Notes and Queries*, 7, 1960, 73–6.

11 *Thomas Hardy's Personal Writings*, ed H. Orel, 1967, 91.

12 Quoted by Schlauch, op cit, 166 (from Barnes's *Glossary of the Dorset Dialect*, Dorchester, 1886).

13 The comments of Ada Lawrence and W. E. Hopkin are quoted in the Viking Critical Library Edition of *Sons and Lovers*, ed J. Moynahan, New York, 1968, 443, 450.

14 K. C. Phillipps, 'Lucy Steele's English', *English Studies*, 1969 Supplement, lv, lxi.

15 Quoted by S. A. Leonard, *The Doctrine of Correctness in English Usage 1700–1800*, Madison, 1929, 176.

16 A. P. Rossiter, *Our Living Language*, 1953, 80–1.

17 Bulwer had noted a similar phenomenon in contemporary speech as early as 1833: writing (in *England and the English*) of the speech of 'the best and most fastidious society', he noted that 'Our rational conversation is for the most part carried on in a series of the most extraordinary and rugged abbreviations – a species of talking shorthand'.

18 Quoted in J. Wildeblood and P. Brinson, *The Polite World*, 1965, 237–8.

19 *Cf* T. Blount, 'Poor Jo, Education, and the Problem of Juvenile Delinquency in Dickens' *Bleak House*', *Modern Philology*, 62, 1965, 338.

20 G. L. Brook, *English Dialects*, 1963, 174.

21 Dickens wrote to Mark Lemon on 20 February 1854, asking him to 'note down and send me any slang terms among the tumblers and circus-people, that you can call to mind ? I have noted down some – I want them in my new story – but it is very probable that you will recall several which I have not got'.

Further references

P. Bentley, *The English Regional Novel*, 1941.

D. P. Costello, 'The Language of *The Catcher in the Rye*', in *Salinger*, ed H. A. Grunwald, 1964, 266–76.

88   SPEECH IN THE ENGLISH NOVEL

W. A. Craigie, 'Dialect in Literature', in *Essays by Divers Hands*, 17, 1938, 69–91.

J. Franklyn, *The Cockney: a Survey of London Life and Language*, 1953.

P. Ingham, 'Dialect in the Novels of Hardy and George Eliot', in *Literary English Since Shakespeare*, ed G. Watson, 1970, 347–63.

S. Ives, 'Dialect Differentiation in the Stories of Joel Chandler Harris', in *Readings in Applied Linguistics*, ed H. B. Allen, New York, 1958.

P. J. Keating, *The Working Classes in Victorian Fiction*, 1971 (Ch 10 is on 'The Phonetic Representation of Cockney').

R. B. Le Page, 'Dialect in West Indian Literature', *Journal of Commonwealth Literature*, 7, 1969, 1–7.

A. McIntosh, *An Introduction to a Survey of Scottish Dialects*, Edinburgh, 1952.

W. Matthews, *Cockney Past and Present*, 1938.

M. Pittock, 'Ivy Compton-Burnett's Use of Dialogue', *English Studies*, 51, 1970, 43–46.

N. Page, 'Convention and Consistency in Dickens' Cockney Dialect', *English Studies*, 51, 1970, 339–44.

E. Partridge, *Dictionary of Slang and Unconventional English*, 1961.

E. Partridge, *Slang Today and Yesterday*, 1933.

R. Quirk, *The Use of English*, 1968, Ch 10.

A. S. C. Ross, 'Linguistic Class-indicators in Present-day English', *Neuphilologische Mitteilungen*, 55, 1954, 20–56.

F. Schmidt, 'A Study in English School-life and School-boy Slang, as Represented by Kipling's *Stalky & Co*', *Englische Studien*, 39, 1908, 240–274.

E. Sivertsen, *Cockney Phonology*, Oslo, 1960.

G. Trease, 'Language in the Historical Novel', *English*, 12, 1959, 126–129.

K. Watson, 'Dinah Morris and Mrs Evans: A Comparative Study of Methodist Diction', *Review of English Studies*, 22, 1971, 282–294.

E. Weekley, 'Mrs Gamp and the King's English', in *Adjectives and Other Words*, 1930.

H. C. Wyld, 'Class Dialect and Standard English', in *A Miscellany Presented to J. M. Mackay*, 1914, 283–291.

The following novels all contain, to a greater or lesser extent, examples of 'dialect speech' in the sense in which that term has been used in this chapter. A much fuller list, though circumscribed both chronologically and by the definition of dialect on which it is based, is L. Leclaire's *A General Analytical Bibliography of the Regional Novelists of the British Isles, 1800–1950*, Paris, 1954.

H. Fielding, *Tom Jones*, 1749.
T. Smollett, *Humphry Clinker*, 1771.
F. Burney, *Evelina*, 1778.
M. Edgeworth, *Castle Rackrent*, 1800.
W. Scott, *Waverley Novels* (*passim*).
C. R. Maturin, *Melmoth the Wanderer*, 1820.
J. Galt, *Annals of the Parish*, 1821; *The Entail*, 1823.
J. G. Lockhart, *Adam Blair*, 1822.
S. Lever, *Charles O'Malley*, 1840.
E. Brontë, *Wuthering Heights*, 1847.

E. C. Gaskell, *Mary Barton*, 1848; *North and South*, 1855.
G. Eliot, *Adam Bede*, 1859.
G. MacDonald, *David Elginbrod*, 1863.
R. D. Blackmore, *Cripps, the Carrier*, 1877.
T. Hardy, *Wessex Novels* (*passim*).
J. M. Barrie, *A Window in Thrums*, 1889.
R. L. Stevenson, *Weir of Hermiston*, 1896.
A. Morrison, *A Child of the Jago*, 1896.
R. Kipling, *Stalky & Co*, 1899; *Kim*, 1901.

M. Bowen, *The Viper of Milan*, 1906.
H. G. Wells, *The History of Mr Polly*, 1910.
A. Bennett, *Clayhanger*, 1910.
D. H. Lawrence, *Sons and Lovers*, 1913.
Neil Munro, *The New Road*, 1914.
L. O'Flaherty, *The Informer*, 1925.
J. B. Priestley, *The Good Companions*, 1929.
H. E. Bates, *The Poacher*, 1935.
W. Holtby, *South Riding*, 1936.
P. G. Wodehouse, *The Code of the Woosters*, 1938.

J. D. Salinger, *The Catcher in the Rye*, 1951.
J. Masters, *Bhowani Junction*, 1954.
A. Tutuola, *My Life in the Bush of Ghosts*, 1954.
C. Achebe, *Things Fall Apart*, 1958
A. Sillitoe, *Saturday Night and Sunday Morning*, 1958.
V. S. Naipaul, *A House for Mr Biswas*, 1961.
S. Chaplin, *The Day of the Sardine*, 1961.
S. Barstow, *Joby*, 1964.
P. Roth, *Portnoy's Complaint*, 1969.

Chapter 4

Speech and character: idiolect

It is probably no exaggeration to say that the speech of any individual is as unique (though not as unchangeable) as his fingerprints. This uniqueness derives from the infinite number of ways in which the features of the spoken language, on the phonological, lexical and grammatical levels, may be combined to form distinguishable modes of utterance or spoken styles. And although written speech, whether a record of actual utterances or a fiction, is necessarily deprived of many of the finer points which make for individual variety in the spoken language, enough possibilities remain for the range of written dialogue to be very wide indeed, and for the differences between individual examples to be almost endless. The features which, in particular combinations, make for uniqueness may be broadly classified under two heads:

[1] those indicating membership of some social or regional or other readily identifiable group – Old Etonians, say, or Anglican clergymen, or Petticoat Lane stallholders, or English-speaking Welshmen; and

[2] those which are personal and idiosyncratic. Professor Higgins, in the first act of Shaw's *Pygmalion*, detected in Colonel Pickering's speech traces of a career which embraced 'Cheltenham, Harrow, Cambridge, and India'; but Pickering's speech inevitably contains certain favourite words and turns of phrase, idiosyncrasies of pronunciation, mannerisms of stress and intonation, and all the other qualities which distinguish the speech of any given upper-middle-class, public-school-and-university-educated, Anglo-Indian ex-soldier from that of other officers and gentlemen with a similar social, educational and occupational background. 'Speech' here is, of course, to be taken as referring not to any individual utterance but to the totality of a user's resources as manifested in the sum of his performances as a speaker; obviously any given sentence may exactly resemble that of another user, but differences will inevitably emerge over a larger stretch of language. Although with a living speaker we have to consider

'competence' as well as 'performance', with fictional and dramatic speech we are in the much more straightforward position of having a limited and complete body of material to study.

A little reflection on the speech habits of one's acquaintance (and one-self) provides plenty of evidence of these two kinds of identifying charac-teristics, the group and the individual. A similar duality is to be found in the dialogue of many fictional characters. The discussion of dialects in the previous chapter has inevitably given an incomplete account of the language of many of the examples cited, and has (for methodological con-venience) ignored the fact that regional and other markers do not con-stitute the whole nature of a character's speech. For there remains an individual factor, responsible for recognizable and significant differences between characters with identical backgrounds. Thus Sam Weller's idiolect is not a carbon copy of that of his father Tony, in spite of common elements; and Nicholas Higgins's speech in *North and South* is carefully distinguished from that of his daughter Bessy. The present chapter is concerned with individual rather than group features, though the dis-tinction is naturally far from being a sharply-defined one.

One may ask the fundamental questions: what kinds of relationship can exist between the speech of a character and that character's total function in the novel? what are the ways in which different kinds of characteriza-tion through speech work, and what are their distinctive effects? We may begin by distinguishing six types of relationship, involving different uses of language. These are not mutually exclusive, nor do they necessarily cover every example that might be found; but they will serve to indicate some basic distinctions which, by being overlooked, have at times caused critical confusion.

[1] Speech as identification: that is, dialogue in which a limited range of easily-recognized characteristics is found. These are often strongly marked and frequently repeated, but usually not significantly developed.

[2] Speech as parody: the use of dialogue in which certain features of speech well-known outside the work of fiction are exaggerated for pur-poses of comedy or satire. This offers more possibility of development and variation than [1], but differs in degree rather than in kind.

[3] Realistic speech: in which an attempt is made to suggest with some precision certain features of speech encountered in real life and appropriate to the character in question, but subject to the qualifications made in earlier chapters with regard to the possibilities of true 'realism' in fic-tional dialogue.

[4] Conventional speech: non-realistic dialogue in which qualities of speech are to be understood as representing, symbolically or metonymically as it were, qualities of character.

[5] Token-speech: the use in dialogue of accepted 'equivalents' to represent features which for some reason cannot be represented realistically.

[6] Neutral speech: stylistically undifferentiated, non-idiosyncratic dialogue which serves some other purpose than contributing to characterization.

Some discussion and illustration of these categories will help to clarify and justify them.

Since the novel is primarily concerned with recording individual experience, the creation of characters with recognizably individual elements has always been regarded as one of the novelist's chief concerns. To the accomplishment of this end, a distinctive mode of speech will usually have much to contribute, and may at times bear the main burden of the task. Historically speaking, the Jonsonian comedy of humours, wherein characters are distinguished according to a ruling passion or dominant trait, was still powerful enough to influence the eighteenth-century novel and to pass into the following century, most obviously from Smollett to Dickens. Nor can we ignore the influence of the theatre on the early novel, for in the light of such influence 'speech as identification' is both the transposition into the newer genre of a device already well-established in stage dialogue, and an attempt by the novel to reproduce, *sui generis*, the effect of an actor's performance of his role. In the theatre, simply by *being* an individual with his own physique, costume, movements, facial and vocal qualities, etc, the actor endows the role he is playing with its own unique individuality. Since the novel can offer no seen presence of this kind, all these manifestations, if they are to have any equivalents, must be conveyed verbally, inside or outside the dialogue; and since dialogue is more dramatic than description or comment, it will often be chosen to perform much of this task of individuation, especially by the novelist who conceives character and incident in dramatic terms. The popularity in the nineteenth century of the serially-published novel gave a fresh impetus to this type of characterization and to the kind of dialogue which often serves its purpose, since the reader's memory needed artificial aids when the reading experience extended over a long period. Complex plots, with extensive character-lists, also encouraged the type of character portrayed in bold and easily-grasped terms. The limitations of the method are as obvious as its advantages: vividness entails the risk of caricature, and instant recognition tends to rule out a more subtle rendering of character. Later novelists and critics have sometimes been scornful of the 'flat' or 'two-dimensional' character which is the product of this method; against this we must set the fact that some of the most memorable characters in fiction belong to this category.

There is also a significant influence of the graphic arts on the early novel (Fielding and Smollett make frequent references to Hogarth), and it is helpful to relate this mode of characterization to visual caricature. When the caricaturist selects a visual feature, he does so as a ready means of asserting the uniqueness (in relation to the context) of the character concerned: thus Cruikshank, in illustrating *Oliver Twist*, presents us with a Fagin who is immediately recognizable on reappearance. The writer performs a very similar task: in the dialogue, a combination of simple features repeated by this character and unshared by others (for example, Fagin's ingratiating form of address 'my dear') gives the reader the pleasure of recognition and the sense of a character who is, in the world of the novel, unique. These repeated signals can take various forms. The most obvious is a favourite word or expression, such as Uriah Heep's use of *umble* in *David Copperfield*. Heep is conceived in terms of Jonsonian simplicity, and this recurring key-word of his conversation is an important clue to the calculated self-abasement which is part of his strategy as plotter and hypocrite. With other characters, it may be not so much a single word as a recurring type of language – as, in the same novel, Mr Micawber's fondness for such flowery Latinisms as 'stipendiary emoluments'. (Again, the habit is a clue to character, this time of foolish optimism and self-deception: a man who can refer to a home as 'domiciliary accommodation' or to marriage as 'the Hymeneal altar' is unlikely to have a sound grasp of reality.) Or the mannerism may be syntactical, as with Jingle in *Pickwick Papers*. A probable source for Jingle is Thomas Holcroft's play *The Road to Ruin* (1792), in which Goldfinch is made to speak in a similar telegraphic style. What is significant, though, is that there is some occupational appropriateness in the source which does not persist in Dickens: Goldfinch has been a jockey before becoming a man-about-town, and his speech seems intended to suggest the staccato utterances natural to a man who has spent his formative years on horseback, but Jingle's speech seems to have no *raison d'être* beyond eccentricity for its own sake. Phonological qualities (like Mr Sleary's lisping pronunciation in *Hard Times*) can be invoked for the same purpose.

Attempts to render more fully the complexities of human individuality virtually banished this kind of dialogue from serious modern novels, but it survives in comic fiction (in, for example, the stories of P. G. Wode-house) and, with unabated popularity, in radio and television enter-tainment.

What has been referred to as 'speech as parody' relies on the reader's previous acquaintance with a recognized mode of speech and his ability to detect this when it is assigned, variously distorted, to a fictional charac-ter. In referring to 'a recognized mode of speech' one needs to dis-tinguish between assumptions based on the reader's experience of life and those derived ultimately from his previous knowledge of fictional or dramatic conventions. Let us consider, by way of illustration, the speech of clergymen. Although a detailed examination of the subject would doubtless reveal many sectarian and other differences, and suggest a whole cluster of sub-groups, there is a sense in which certain qualities – lexical, syntactical and (most obviously, perhaps) phonological – are associated with this professional group broadly considered. Since a clergyman's vocation pervades his entire life to a greater extent than that of (say) an accountant or a butcher, it is not surprising that his speech behaviour on private or informal occasions should be influenced by the linguistic and vocal habits he has developed in the course of his professional training and experience. In literature, these qualities are both simplified and high-lighted for specific effects; yet the writer depends on the reader's capacity to recognize certain features of speech as tokens of a man's calling and to respond to dialogue in accordance with the extent to which these signals are presented 'straight' or with comic or satiric exaggeration or distor-tion. Several examples from different novelists will suggest the range of effects that are possible, and will indicate incidentally that 'parody' as used in this context is not an exclusively humorous device.

The unworldly Parson Adams in Fielding's *Joseph Andrews* is given a form of speech which, even in the most mundane and even farcical en-counters of daily life, recalls the Bible and the pulpit. The distinctive effect is achieved partly by a higher average sentence-length and a greater form-ality of syntax than in the dialogue of many characters with whom Adams comes into contact, and partly by a deliberate archaism of grammar and vocabulary: he uses, for instance, the old-fashioned second-person singular as well as such biblical and literary words as *peradventure* and *surcease*. His manner is consistent, both in set speeches such as the sermon on patience delivered to Joseph (IV, 8) and in his conversations with others speaking a much more familiar and colloquial idiom. Adams's speech appears to embody a clear purpose on Fielding's part: to combine an impression of moral dignity with an unworldliness which is often comic in its results if not in its nature. A later example probably owing a debt to Fielding is that of the Rev Josiah Crawley in Trollope's *Last Chronicle of Barset*. Like Adams, Crawley hardly distinguishes in his speech between public and private occasions, or between the church and the market-place or draw-ing-room; the results are often comically incongruous, as when he tells Mr Toogood, the worldly London lawyer, that '"it seemeth to me that you are a messenger of glad tidings, whose feet are beautiful upon the mountains"'. More overtly satiric is Jane Austen's Mr Collins in *Pride and Prejudice*: like the previous examples, Collins is formal, even pedantic, on informal occasions, but he lacks the moral dignity which atones for such eccentricity. In his speech we find not the genuine solemnity of Crawley's periods but a hollow and pretentious addiction to stock ex-pressions of biblical or literary origin ('olive branch', 'humble abode', etc) – a reliable index of his commonplace mind.

Finally, the most elaborate of the examples is characteristically from Dickens: that of Mr Chadband, the preacher of 'no particular denomina-tion' in *Bleak House*. Chadband is distinguished not only by his speech but by an expressive gesture: he 'never speaks without first putting up his great hand, as delivering a token to his hearers that he is going to edify them', and this assertiveness finds verbal equivalents in his speech. As with many of Dickens's comic and satiric characters, conversation gives place to monologue and the distinctions between public and private utterance are obscured. Chadband has a marked fondness for framing his harangues on the model of a catechism, for parallelism, for fluent and repetitive catalogues of items, including lists of synonyms, for the form of address 'my friends' (at once ingratiating and patronising), for archaisms and other words with biblical associations (*behold* for *see*, *stumbled* for *sinned*, etc), for biblical quotations such as 'a still small voice' and pseudo-quotations such as 'like the thirsty swallow', and – unlike the three other examples cited – for clerical pronunciations orthographically rendered (*untoe*, *terewth*, etc). Chadband's first speech is typical:

> "My friends," says Mr Chadband, "Peace be on this house! On the master thereof, on the mistress thereof, on the young maidens, and on the young men! My friends, why do I wish for peace? What is peace? Is it war? Is it strife? No. Is it lovely, and gentle, and beautiful, and pleasant, and serene, and joyful? O yes! . . ."

The question-and-answer method parodied here was commonplace in evangelical publications of the period, and it is entirely appropriate that Chadband should, quite literally, speak like a book.

Although Dickens's first readers may have recognized in Chadband certain linguistic habits observable in actual members of their own society, his method is unmistakably one of exaggeration, and 'realism' – even in the relative sense in which the term is used throughout this study – hardly one of his concerns. For we require of 'realistic speech' that it should not offend our sense of the probable or surprise by a fine excess: its virtues, indeed, are at least as much negative as positive. One kind of realistic dialogue has already been discussed and illustrated in Chapter 3, since the various devices used to indicate regional and other affiliations represent an attempt to suggest resemblances between fictional speech and that of real life. One must quickly add, of course – what indeed was made clear by some of the examples given – that the operation of convention is capable of modifying the observed features of actual speech, on occasions quite drastically. Or the term might be used, again relatively, to assert a degree of difference between two examples of dialogue: thus, to invoke the names of novelists whose work has already been referred to, one might plausibly characterize the dialogue of Muriel Spark as more realistic than that of Ivy Compton-Burnett; and the judgment, so far from resting on merely subjective impressions, could readily be reinforced by analysis of lexical, syntactical and other features and comparison of these in each case with the known features of actual speech. 'Realism' remains, however – and especially as applied to dialogue – an unsatisfactory and rather unhelpful concept. What needs to be stressed is not so much the nature of speech as an autonomous phenomenon as its relationship to a novelist's total purpose; and, in the light of this contextual assessment, 'realistic' speech will be seen as in no way intrinsically and necessarily superior to more conventional or stylized varieties, merely as more appropriate to some kinds of fiction, or to some elements within a novel, than to others.

In a particular instance, a novelist may decline to give to a character the form of speech which is suggested as appropriate by his social and other attributes. Realism, it would seem, can be inhibited by a conflict between the moral status of the character in the novel – as hero or heroine, for example – and the associations and expectations normally aroused by the kind of speech that realistic considerations might demand (though these associations and expectations are not, of course, constant but themselves reflect the assumptions and prejudices of a particular audience). Plausibility will then yield place to convention; and the result of this substitution of one kind of dialogue for another may be referred to as 'conventional speech' or 'heroic speech'. For nineteenth-century novelists what was involved was often the imposing of a standard of 'correct'

English upon characters who enjoy a certain moral status and who seem intended to elicit a response of moral approbation from the reader. The fact that this 'correctness' may be at variance with what is revealed of their social, educational and regional background has sometimes caused a good deal of concern and confusion among literary critics. Turning again for familiar and relevant illustrations to the novels of Dickens, let us examine selected examples in detail. Two characters, one from an early and the other from a late novel, will exemplify Dickens's apparent assumption that it is, if not impossible, at any rate very difficult to create an impression of dignity and moral worth in a character speaking an idiom which departs from standard usage, and his use of the convention whereby speech is determined not by environmental factors but by innate moral qualities.

The problem was confronted early in the novelist's career, since it is one of two main directions in which, in *Oliver Twist*, he ventures upon the exploration of what is for him fresh linguistic territory. (The other, the rendering of the speech of the criminal classes, will be discussed later in this chapter.) We have in this novel an early example of the devising of what may be styled a 'language fit for heroes to speak'. The problem is raised most acutely when Oliver enters the world of the Artful Dodger and Bill Sikes, where he is affected neither morally nor linguistically by the taint of their society. On the other hand, he is in more than one sense completely at home in the middle-class establishment of Mr Brownlow, where there is no sense of incongruity between the speech of the workhouse orphan and his well-to-do benefactor, whereas at Fagin's he inhabits a foreign country, where cant expressions must be translated into standard English for his benefit. Earlier, his genteel locutions "I beg your pardon, Sir . . . did you knock?") are contrasted with the crude utterances of Noah Claypole, who ironically enough taunts the well-spoken Oliver with his low origins ('. . . . my work'us brat!'); and the difference between them is plainly one of sensibility and moral worth rather than environment as a determinant of speech behaviour. For with Oliver's linguistic correctness goes an inviolable moral sense, which he has not learned in the workhouse, any more than he has acquired his speech habits there; and these two manifestations of essential gentility find a meeting-point in such utterances as the following:

"Oh! pray have mercy on me, and do not make me steal. For the love of all the bright angels that rest in Heaven, have mercy upon me!"

Dickens's conception of appropriate speech is thus quite different from that of a later novelist such as E. M. Forster: in *Howards End*, for instance, Leonard Bast speaks quite differently from the Schlegels and the Wilcoxes because of his different social origins and educational opportunities, but Oliver speaks like a gentleman *in spite of* his workhouse origins. Environment may, in real life, be the determinant of speech habits, but for the purposes of his fiction Dickens has decided that blood and virtue shall be allowed to shine through, just as Perdita speaks blank verse even in the shepherd's cottage. Nor is the comparison with romantic drama a merely idle one, for the alternative to considering such phenomena as Oliver's speech as artistic flaws is to regard the works in which they occur as belonging to a genre different in some important respects from the realistic novel.

A recent critic, Steven Marcus, touching briefly on 'well-bred speech as indicative of inborn virtue', connects Dickens's use of this convention with his experiences in the blacking warehouse, where he was himself (in his own words) the 'young gentleman' among the boys who, though working by his side, nevertheless seem to have recognized him instinctively as their superior. Marcus also comments that, in this novel, 'goodness and wickedness seem to live in quite separate regions',[1] and it may be said that this sense of separateness is conveyed to a considerable extent by linguistic contrasts. Where commerce between the regions of good and evil does take place, notably involving the hero, the essential difference between them is stressed by the use of a convention of dialogue which deliberately sacrifices realism to moral appropriateness. Dickens claimed in his Preface that the character of Oliver shows 'the principle of Good surviving through every adverse circumstance, and triumphing at last', and it would clearly be alien to such a conception of character to demand that Oliver's speech should accurately reflect his upbringing.

At the other end of Dickens's career, Lizzie Hexam in *Our Mutual Friend* offers a more complex case-study, and several recent critics have been a good deal concerned over the apparent disparity between her background and her speech. Philip Hobsbaum finds the transformation of the child of the streets and the waterside into a middle-class heroine unconvincing: he comments that Dickens's decision to take his heroine 'from the lowest and most illiterate classes . . . would have more point if her behaviour and accent were less resolutely that of a middle-class heroine', and quotes from a scene in the last section of the novel to justify his comment. Kenneth Muir expresses puzzlement at Lizzie's command of standard English:

It was part of Dickens's purpose to show that the illiterate Lizzie, brought up in a foul slum . . . could display a moral delicacy, heroism and self-sacrifice superior to that shown by any of the characters drawn from a higher class. Quite unrealistically, even when talking to Jenny Wren, she apparently speaks the Queen's English; and when Eugene falls in love with her, he is very conscious of the difference of class, but not of her speech . . .

R. C. Churchill refers to the 'incredible figures of Lizzie Hexam and Eugene Wrayburn', describing the former as 'one of the worst examples of the misplaced heroic', and quoting A. W. Ward as saying that Lizzie 'has to discard the colour of her surroundings and talk the conventional dialect as well as express the conventional sentiments of the heroic world'.[2]

One might reflect that such criticisms constitute a somewhat oblique tribute to Dickens for his boldness in creating a heroine of unconventional social status. Against all this, however, may be set a comment of Kathleen Tillotson, who (though not referring specifically to *Our Mutual Friend*) sees Little Dorrit, like Oliver Twist and Little Nell, as representing the idea of

the strength and indestructibility of natural, innocent virtue . . . her goodness, with such an upbringing, may be thought implausible; but it must be seen as expressing what still survived of Dickens's own indestructible faith – expressing it almost allegorically, with the validity of fairy tale.[3]

In this class, Lizzie may perhaps also claim a place; and just as it is unreasonable to entertain expectations of realistic dialogue in fairytale and allegory, so we may to some extent have to reconsider our expectations in approaching Dickens's novel, and ask ourselves whether attitudes derived from a reading of realistic fiction are entirely appropriate.

Although there is fairly obviously a Lizzie Hexam problem, it will be argued here that it is by no means as extreme or as incapable of solution as some of the views already quoted seem to imply. It is perfectly possible that the evidence of the text does not provide full support for the animadversions of such critics as Muir and Churchill, who are conceivably recollecting specific scenes from the middle and later sections of the novel, rather than viewing the *total* presentation of Lizzie's speech throughout the twelve chapters of the novel in which she makes an appearance. Dickens was in fact at some pains in her early appearances to mark her speech as deviating noticeably from standard English in some respects. Lizzie's speech is, therefore, not a constant, but develops as her character itself develops, particularly through her relationship with Wrayburn and

Headstone, and as she takes her place as heroine – a role which is by no means unambiguously announced at the outset. Speech is presented in the novel – and not only in relation to Lizzie – as one of the facets of social behaviour which are the correlates of social class; and class-consciousness is itself one of the themes of the novel. It may, then, be argued that Dickens is not so much giving his heroine a ready-made idiom that happens to come to hand, as making her speech and the changes it undergoes an index of her development. To justify this view, it will be necessary to look in some detail at her successive appearances. And because one of the themes of the novel is, as already suggested, class-consciousness and class-mobility – a preoccupation manifest not only in the Veneerings and their circle, the Podsnaps, the Boffins and the Wilfers, but (more relevantly to the present instance) in the two rivals for Lizzie's love – it will be necessary to consider her speech, and the kind of status it implies, not as an isolated phenomenon but in the light of these relationships.

An examination of her earliest appearances suggests that there may be some exaggeration in the views of her speaking only 'the Queen's English' or 'the conventional dialect . . . of the heroic world.' At this stage she is in fact relatively taciturn: in Chapter 1 she accompanies her father on the river as a mainly silent witness of his ghastly occupation, uttering only three short speeches – twenty-eight words in all – in the course of the chapter. She talks more freely to her brother in Chapter 3, and there are various indications of the homely quality of her speech, which includes such forms as *a'most, a-looking, of an evening, in revenge-like,* and such a sentence as the following:

> "I was all in a tremble of another sort when you owned to father you could write a little."

It is in the same chapter that the theme of social mobility through education is first mooted: whereas the father's illiteracy is stressed ("'I can't read, nor I don't want to it . . .'"), the son's case is very different: his 'writing, though large and round, was good', and Charley's prospective rise into another social class is already apparent. This difference is sharply reflected in their speech: that of Gaffer Hexam is abundantly marked with indications of uneducated pronunciation and non-standard grammatical forms, whereas the boy's, though not yet so free from grammatical faults as it will later become, is unmarked by deviant spellings. Two brief quotations will illustrate the contrast between, respectively, father and son:

"'Taint not to say here, but it's close by. I do everything reg'lar. I've giv' notice of the circumstarnce to the police, and the police have took possession of it. No time ain't been lost, on any hand . . ."

"It's a goodish stretch, sir. I come up in a cab, and the cab's waiting to be paid. We could go back in it before you paid it, if you like. I went first to your office, according to the direction of the papers found in the pockets, and there I see nobody but a chap of about my age who sent me on here."

Lizzie's third appearance shows her addressing the tavern proprietress as 'Miss' (as will emerge shortly, forms of address are employed with some subtlety in the depicting of her changing status), and she again addresses her father in homely idiom:

"The meat's ready now, father. Eat it while it's hot and comfortable."

We then, apart from a single very brief appearance, see no more of Lizzie for another eleven chapters. Book II opens with chapters titled 'Of an Educational Character' and 'Still Educational', and her social and educational progress now becomes one of the main features of her development. Headstone's attraction to her is at this stage somewhat moderated by awareness of the limitations of her background: '"I suppose – your sister – . . . has received hardly any teaching, Hexam?"' He realizes that, from a careerist's point of view, a match with Lizzie might be very much improved on; and he is hypersensitively conscious of class differences and the gulf between the Hexam family and the level to which, by his own exertions, he has raised himself – a feeling that will later give ironical effectiveness to Wrayburn's gibes at the schoolmaster's status, and his deliberately insulting use of 'Schoolmaster' as a form of address.

Headstone prompts Charley to suggest that he, the schoolmaster, should undertake to have Lizzie taught in order to qualify her for a rise in status: as often, Dickens stresses the power of education as an instrument of social mobility. A few pages later Wrayburn arrives at the same decision, and proposes to pay for her to be given 'certain instruction', of the value of which she must be fully aware: '"You know that it's good to have it, or you would never have so devoted yourself to your brother's having it."' Here, tribute is paid to the power of education by – strikingly enough – a member of the privileged classes; and it is in the context of these questions of educational opportunity and awareness of status that the change in Lizzie's speech must be viewed.

At this stage her relationship to the two men who are taking an interest in her is still that of an inferior to her acknowledged betters: she calls both 'sir', and is ruefully conscious of being at a disadvantage in speaking to the effortlessly eloquent Eugene: '"It's not easy for me to talk to you . . . for you see all the consequences of what I say, as soon as I say it."' In her next major appearance, however (Bk II, Ch 11), she begins to display both the moral dignity of a heroine and the command of language that can adequately give verbal expression to this quality. The scene in question contains a dialogue with Headstone in which be begins to reveal the strength of his passion for Lizzie and his jealousy of his upper-class rival; and Lizzie herself shows here a firmness of purpose and a refusal to be intimidated that reflect a growing self-confidence. Significantly, the form of address she employs now changes from 'sir', used twice at the beginning of the scene, to 'Mr Headstone', used five times in the latter part with an effect of cold dignity and even reproof, after he has revealed his attitude to Wrayburn: 'she answered him very steadily'. It would be wrong to suppose, however, that Dickens has abruptly transformed the reticent Lizzie into a model of self-confident eloquence: she speaks comparatively little in the course of this scene, her total contribution to the dialogue amounting to almost exactly one-third of that of her interlocutor, and a good part of it being contained in a single speech. But the emphasis in the novelist's intention has clearly shifted: there are no further reminders of her lowly origins in the form of homely expressions or occasional orthographic indications of uneducated pronunciation; she now speaks standard English, though of a plain and unadorned variety. The contrast in this scene is not between the schoolmaster and the illiterate, but between two temperaments, and the need to assert *moral* status has for the novelist assumed priority over considerations of realism, since the representation of the speech of a girl whose education is as yet incomplete (though she has clearly made progress in this direction) would hardly have served the purpose of making a heroine of Lizzie.

The same considerations are maintained in her next interview with Headstone (Ch 15), where her simple but fearless declarations contrast strongly with the growingly obsessive quality of his speech, his abnormal emotional state being conveyed by extensive use of repetition and parallelism in his utterances, whilst the expression of his passionate feelings in coherent and carefully-structured sentences indicates the tremendous self-control he is exerting. Compare, for instance, her quiet protestation:

"Mr Headstone, I have heard enough. Let me stop you here. It will be better for you and better for me. Let us find my brother."

with the subsequent speech of Headstone which includes such passages
as

> "You could draw me to fire, you could draw me to water, you could
> draw me to the gallows, you could draw me to any death, you could
> draw me to anything I have most avoided, you could draw me to any
> exposure and disgrace . . ."

There is also a minor but interesting piece of manuscript evidence bearing on the form of address used by Lizzie in speaking to Bradley. Her
repeated use of his name and title ('Mr Headstone') perhaps points to the
distance which, by establishing and maintaining an element of formality in
their relationship, she hopes to keep between them. In one place, however,
the manuscript shows that at the point where her own strong feelings
lead her to abandon restraint and reproach him in forceful terms, the
name, though originally written, was cancelled on second thoughts: the
relevant sentence reads

> "You asked me to hear you out [Mr Headstone] and you will not
> speak."

The cancellation adds to the dramatic effectiveness by implying, in the
final version, that Lizzie momentarily abandons, in the intensity of her
indignation, the coldly courteous manner she has prescribed for herself.

Another contrast in personalities in which differences in both social
and moral status are seen to operate is provided by the conversation between Lizzie and Bella in the ninth chapter of Book III. Lizzie's serious
and modest manner is emphasized by contrast with its antithesis, Bella's
'wayward, playful, affectionate nature, giddy for want of the weight of
some sustaining purpose, and capricious because it was always fluttering
among little things'. That the contrast was for Dickens the main point of
the scene is shown by his manuscript note in the plan for the thirteenth
number: 'Lizzie to work an influence on Bella's character at its wavering
point' (underlined twice) and again in a separate note on this chapter:
'Bella persuaded to contrast herself with Lizzie.' The speeches in which
the girls make reference to the men who love them will illustrate that this
contrast is exemplified plainly enough by their speech:

1 "Well! Perhaps one," said Bella. "I am sure I don't know. I *had* one,
  but what he may think about it at the present time, I can't say. Perhaps
  I have half a one (of course I don't count that Idiot, George Sampson).
  However, never mind me. I want to hear about you."

2 "There is a certain man," said Lizzie, "a passionate and angry man, who says he loves me, and who I must believe does love me. He is the friend of my brother. I shrank from him within myself when my brother first brought him to me; but the last time I saw him, he terrified me more than I can say."

Bella's impulsive manner of speech is conveyed by short sentences; her idiom is colloquial from the outset, whilst Lizzie's is formal at first but becomes somewhat less so as the relationship between the two girls develops. Again, the difference between them is partly marked by the forms of address employed: from her first words, Bella refers to the other as 'Lizzie,' 'dear' and 'my dear', whilst to Lizzie she only becomes 'my dear' in the last part of the scene, after their intimacy has become established. Similarly, in a later dialogue with Wrayburn (Bk IV, Ch 6), though he calls her 'Lizzie' from the start, he is 'Mr Wrayburn' to her throughout, marking the social contrast between them – a contrast at one point made quite explicit:

"It is impossible, Mr Wrayburn. How can I think of you as being on equal terms with me?"

There follows her rescue of Eugene and their subsequent marriage; and it is only *after* the ceremony that she uses his Christian name for the first time – a point whose significance is not intended to be lost upon the reader. Her use of his name is credited with almost supernatural power, calling him back from the unconsciousness that threatens him as he hovers between life and death:

". . . speak to me by my name, and I think I shall come back."
"Yes, dear Eugene."
"There!" he exclaimed, smiling. "I should have gone then but for that!"

This is the climax of Lizzie's role in the novel, and apart from a brief appearance in the penultimate chapter, her part is concluded. It has been pointed out that this is the only occasion on which Dickens marries a low-born heroine to a man of the upper classes, but Lizzie has fitted herself to be Wrayburn's wife not only by her heroism but by the increase in self-confidence and self-awareness which her moral courage in the face of adversity has nurtured; and this development, extending throughout almost the whole compass of the novel, is at intervals accompanied by markers – unobtrusive but not insignificant – of the corresponding changes in her use of language. In other words, the modifications in her idiom reflect the growth of her character, which is itself plausibly and sensitively rendered in the course of the book.

To return, in the light of these comments, to the observations quoted earlier from critics of *Our Mutual Friend:* a good deal of the uneasiness that Lizzie's speech seems to have caused stems from an approach that not only disregards some of the evidence of the novel, but also misses an important point – that Lizzie (who is certainly not unique in this respect) belongs to the class of fairy-tale heroines whose rags and squalid surroundings conceal only temporarily an innate excellence, and on whose lips realistic speech would be disconcertingly out of place. At the same time, however, Dickens has made the concession to realism of laying the ground in her early appearances for the development of her speech, which is accompanied by a development in moral stature. We are shown the point from which she starts, and in the early chapters she is certainly far from being Professor Hobsbaum's 'middle-class' heroine.

If Dickens rejects realism in favour of convention in the language of his heroes and heroines, he also does so – though for a somewhat different reason – in the language of his ruffians and villains. Parallel to the assumption that fine speech can serve to indicate a noble nature is the assumption (no doubt more soundly based) that moral turpitude can be suggested through foul speech. At this point, however, for the Victorian novelist the unwritten laws of censorship began to operate; and the writer often finds himself forced into another convention of dialogue, that of 'token-speech'.

The term 'token-speech' is utilized here to refer to the use of conventional and generally accepted substitutes for items in dialogue which would, in their 'straight' form, be regarded as unacceptable at a given time. The canons of unacceptability are largely determined by public taste – and by publishers and editors acting on behalf of the public – and can therefore not be expected to operate with equal force in all periods. The modern novelist writing for adult readers is unlikely to have to resort to token-speech, though radio and television programmes can provide examples, and the convention still proves useful to those writing for specialized audiences – in children's books, for example, or women's magazines of the more conservative kind. Fictional schoolboys, to take an obvious example, are considerably more chaste in their language than real ones; and writers such as (on different levels) Kipling and Frank Richards who have sought to give an impression of the picturesqueness of schoolboy speech without offending the reader – or, more properly, his parents – have been driven to resort to highly stylized dialogue as a result. Earlier, R. L. Stevenson had felt the same constraints when he was at work on *Treasure Island*, originally serialized in a magazine titled *Young Folks*. He wrote to W. E. Henley in 1881 that '. . . the trouble is to work it off without oaths. Buccaneers without oaths – bricks without straw. But youth and the fond parient [*sic*] have to be consulted'.[4] Working it off without oaths had already been a problem for at least half a century, and not only in writing intended mainly for the young. It is true that, earlier, the eighteenth-century novelists had enjoyed a refreshingly tolerant audience, and their writing is correspondingly frank. Smollett's novels in particular are a rich mine of oaths and curses both general and specialized, doubtless derived from his wide experience as doctor, naval surgeon and traveller.[5] With Sterne and the advent of sentimentality in the novel, the attitude becomes more coy; and by the turn of the century, as the manners of society become more refined and the novel itself seeks a wider audience, frankness becomes markedly inhibited. Scott's novels are suitable for reading aloud in the family circle, and Jane Austen's gentlemen are shown speaking only in the presence of ladies. It is true that some of the Regency novelists were prepared to show swearing as still normal among gentlemen of the better class: Maria Edgeworth's *Belinda* (1801), for instance, which Jane Austen admired warmly, is much freer in its dialogue than anything in the latter's work.

Nevertheless, by the time that Queen Victoria came to the throne, the climate of public morality, insofar as it affected a writer's freedom of speech, was already changing. Much of Dickens's success in *Pickwick* was owed to the fact that he hit upon a combination of the contemporary novel of high spirits with the wide acceptability of Scott's work, and was thus enabled to inherit the latter's public. In the Preface to the 1838 edition of *Pickwick* he refers to his trust that 'throughout his book, no incident or expression occurs which could call a blush into the most delicate cheek' – an interesting anticipation of the attitude he was to satirize nearly thirty years later as Podsnappery. The Preface to the third edition of *Oliver Twist* three years later defends the presentation of criminal and immoral characters:

> I saw no reason, when I wrote this book, why the very dregs of life, so long as their speech did not offend the ear, should not serve the purpose of a moral at least as well as its froth and cream.

'So long as their speech did not offend the ear': in this saving clause, Dickens cheerfully renounces the claims of realism and admits the operation of a silent censorship in the writing of his dialogue. A testimonial to his success in simultaneously running with the hares of realism and hunting with the hounds of propriety is provided by a contemporary reviewer in the *Observer*, who wrote that 'The vernacular idiom is given in all its truth and richness, yet free from grossness'. The paradox appears to have been unconscious, yet 'all its truth and richness' is surely short of the truth. As often, Dickens's art is that of the illusionist, and dialogue which appears to give an impression of authenticity is often found on closer examination to be highly conventional in nature, resting on the principles of selection, omission and modification.

To pursue *Oliver Twist* as a familiar case in point: a recent editor has noted 'the gradual elimination of many oaths throughout all texts as the novel left the pages of a man's magazine for an audience including females and "Young Persons".'[6] This is evidence of Dickens's continuing awareness of the power of Mrs Grundy; it also reminds us that the Victorian novelist was exceptionally conscious of the composition, tastes and prejudices of his audience, and that what might be acceptable in one kind of publication was taboo in another. (Later in the century Hardy was to encounter a similar phenomenon, notably over *Tess of the D'Urbervilles*.) Dickens was occupied with the task of mildly bowdlerizing *Oliver Twist*, on and off, for some thirty years, for shortly before his death, when he prepared the reading version *Sikes and Nancy*, he found it advisable to soften some of Sikes's imprecations, 'Hell's fire' being omitted, and 'Damme' becoming 'Hallo'. It has often been pointed out that whereas Nancy, as a streetwalker, would have been familiar with the coarsest language, her speech in the novel is irreproachably chaste; and though, looking back over one's memories of the novel, one can easily think of Sikes's language as being larded with oaths, the impression of heavy swearing is given without the actual use of oaths. Dickens achieves this effect in two ways. One is by the avoidance of direct speech in favour of a narrative statement that fearful (but unspecified) oaths were used (*eg*, 'with a tremendous oath', 'with a hideous imprecation'); the other is to formulate a system of oath-substitutes, picturesque rather than plausible. Thus Sikes is given such expressions as ' Wolves tear your throats!' and 'You white-livered hound!' A more extreme instance is the following remarkable sentence, in which Dickens's debt to the melodramatic stage is apparent:

"If he was left alive till I came, I'd grind his skull under the iron heel of my boot into as many grains as there are hairs upon his head."
(Ch 47)

A similar influence is at work in the speech of a more genteel villain, Ralph Nickleby:

"One word!" cried Ralph, foaming at the mouth . . . "My curse, my bitter, deadly curse, upon you, boy!"   [*Nicholas Nickleby*, Ch 54]

Surviving manuscripts provide many other examples of Dickens's usually scrupulous self-censorship: when an oath – even interpreting that term very broadly – escapes from his pen, Dickens usually catches it, either in revising his manuscript or in correcting his proofs. Thus Fagin's phrase 'You young hounds' originally read 'You young devils'; the convict's 'Damned' in *Great Expectations* was changed to 'Darn me' at the proof stage; and in *Bleak House* 'God only knows' becomes 'It is impossible to say', and the apparently innocent 'God bless you' and 'Lord bless me!' become 'Thank you' and 'O dear me'. Dickens's treatment of this problem, which hardly exists for a modern writer, shows a consciousness of its importance which grows rather than diminishes as the nineteenth century proceeds. The writer for a mixed family audience, which might well include those 'country clergymen's daughters' of whom Leslie Stephen found it necessary to remind Hardy early in his career, had to ask himself not so much 'What kind of language is appropriate?' as 'What kind is acceptable?' As so often, we find dialogue forced into convention and compromise; and for the novelist who is unwilling or unable to shelve the problem completely, a form of dialogue is devised (of which the examples from Bill Sikes are a fair example) whereby certain kinds of speech are given the task of representing, metaphorically or analogically as it were, a language of violence, coarseness or profanity to which they bear little or no literal resemblance.

'Neutral' or undifferentiated speech, the nature of which is negative rather than positive, requires little comment or illustration.[7] It may be thought of as dialogue in which the writer's primary purpose is to convey information rather than to develop character – the 'information', that is to say, relating to other concerns than characterization. If a novelist neglects opportunities to individualize the speakers in his dialogue, this must not be taken to be necessarily a matter for reproach: in kinds of fiction in which plot and action take precedence, dialogue which exhibits considerable intrinsic interest may be a disadvantage. (Detective fiction is, in some of its varieties, a case in point.) Naturally its incidence varies very much from writer to writer: just as dialogue occupies a greater proportion of space in some novels than in others, its diversity may be greater or less; and to say that Trollope, for instance, uses 'neutral' speech much more frequently than Dickens is not to imply that he is necessarily a lesser novelist, though it does perhaps imply that the characterization of the latter is more varied, and the individual episodes generally more dramatic than with the former.

If one proposes, for convenience of discussion, such categories as those already described, this is not to suggest that what we encounter in the course of a novel is a uniform and immutable idiom reserved for a particular character. Indeed, the example of Lizzie Hexam has already shown that development and modification are possible. Change may occur simply in the interests of novelty and variety, as the writer becomes more fully aware of the possibilities of a mode of dialogue which he has perhaps initiated somewhat tentatively. Or changes may mirror a temporary or permanent modification of dramatic function, belonging less to dialogue as an end in itself than to purposes more organically connected with the total intention of the work. Some further examples may be briefly adduced to illustrate both kinds of 'deliberate inconsistency'.

Flora Finching in Dickens's *Little Dorrit* represents a development of a type of speech Dickens had caricatured earlier in Mrs Nickleby, who is described as talking 'in one unbroken monotonous flow, perfectly satisfied to be talking, and caring very little whether anybody listened or not'. The much more richly diversified and comic speech of Flora is characterized most obviously by the disappearance of the sentence as a unit of expression: we are told that 'she never once came to a full stop', and indeed her speech carries to extremes the sound linguistic observation that 'The sentence, as defined for the written language, does not exist'. Since her dialogue is communicated through the written language, Dickens necessarily takes certain liberties with the normal conventions of written prose. Initially this amounts to little more than the omission of some of the customary marks of punctuation:

> "But if we talk of not having changed," said Flora ... "look at Papa, is not Papa precisely what he was when you went away, isn't it cruel and unnatural of Papa to be such a reproach to his own child, if we go on in this way much longer people who don't know us will begin to suppose that I am Papa's Mama!" (I, 13)

Eccentricity here does not infect the syntax, but goes no further than the substitution of commas for full stops and question marks. Soon, however, her habit of switching from one subject to another without warning, of moving from present to past and back again, and of freely interrupting her own discourse with parentheses and interjections combine to produce a more elaborate idiolect. In later chapters she is shown as apt to distort syntax with long digressions and to collocate lexical items incongruously, as in the following:

> "If Fancy's fair dreams," she began, "have ever pictured that when Arthur – cannot overcome it pray excuse me – was restored to freedom even a pie as far from flaky as the present and so deficient in kidney as to be in that respect like a minced nutmeg might not prove unacceptable if offered by the hand of true regard such visions have for ever fled and all is cancelled but being aware that tenderer relations are in contemplation beg to state that I heartily wish well to both. . ." (II, 34)

– and so on, in similar vein, for another ninety words before reaching a full stop.

A simple but striking example of modified speech is provided by Dennis, the hangman and ringleader of the rioters in *Barnaby Rudge*. In his early appearances he is presented as a conventional enough villain, whose foul language (necessarily described rather than illustrated) is picturesque more than offensive, and whose rough treatment of the Queen's English is a natural counterpart of his rough nature:

> "Ha ha!" roared the fellow, smiting his leg; "for a gentleman as 'ull say a pleasant thing in a pleasant way, give me Muster Gashford agin' all London and Westminster! My lord an't a bad 'un at that . . ." (Ch 37)

At the end of the novel, however, as he faces execution, the dramatic situation brings about a startling change in his speech:

> "All I ask, sir – all I want and beg, is time, to make it sure," cried the trembling wretch . . . "The King and Government can't know it's me; or they never would bring me to this dreadful slaughter-house. They know my name, but they don't know it's the same man. Stop my execution – for charity's sake stop my execution, gentlemen . . ." (Ch 77)

In spite of Dr Johnson, it is hard to accept that the imminent prospect of death could have the effect of refining a ruffian's speech: the explanation seems to be that Dickens abandons the orthographic and other indications of uneducated speech at this point, and introduces such middle-class language as 'this dreadful slaughter-house' and 'for charity's sake', in order to raise the character's dramatic status and to avoid marring the seriousness of the episode.

Other examples may be found in *Great Expectations* and *Our Mutual Friend*. In the former, Joe Gargery's speech will be found to change significantly in the course of a single scene (in Chapter 27, on the occasion of his visit to Pip in London). In the early part of the chapter, the comic absurdity of his language, and its contrast to the middle-class English of Pip, are stressed:

> "Which you have that growed," said Joe, "and that swelled, and that gentle-folked ... as to be sure you are a honour to your king and country."

However, indications of uneducated usage virtually disappear later in the scene, in a monologue of some length in which Joe's natural dignity and sensitivity are manifested:

> "You won't find half so much fault in me if you think of me in my forge dress, with my hammer in my hand, or even my pipe. You won't find half so much fault in me if, supposing as you should ever wish to see me, you come and put your head in at the forge window and see Joe the blacksmith, there, at the old anvil, in the old burnt apron, sticking to the old work ..."

As the tone of the scene deepens and Joe is seen not as a buffoon but as a man with a fine moral nature, his language undergoes a corresponding change: the irregular grammatical forms and mispronunciations disappear, and his sentences take on new structures and rhythms. They also increase significantly in length, from an average of about nine and a half words in the first eleven speeches of the scene to about twenty-one words in the monologue from which an extract has been given. In *Our Mutual Friend*, Mr Boffin's speech undergoes a more permanent transformation which suggests that Dickens may have modified his original conception of this character's role. The malapropisms and comic mispronunciations in Boffin's early speeches very largely disappear in the latter part of the novel as he changes from an eccentric of minor importance to a dramatic figure in his own right.

The examples offered in this chapter have suggested that the relationship between dialogue and character-development can be of many different kinds, and that the amount of information relevant to characterization and conveyed by dialogue can vary considerably. The two extremes are represented by dialogue which merely acts as a convenient and palatable medium for the conveying of necessary material to the reader, and that in which the speech of given characters is allowed to develop an independent and often brilliant life without contributing to the larger purposes of the fiction: that is, between dialogue which is merely an alternative and formally distinct kind of narrative, and dialogue as an end in itself. Neither of these, if permitted to dominate large stretches of the novel, is likely to be ultimately satisfactory; and the best examples of dialogue are usually found to contain an intrinsic vitality (an important ingredient in which consists of stylistic features distinguishing it from other elements in the novel) and a purposive quality related to the writer's total intention. A familiar case in point is Miss Bates in Jane Austen's *Emma*: her speeches may appear at first sight to be a self-sufficient eccentricity, 'comic relief', or a verbal *tour de force* inessential to the main business of the novel; yet, as Mary Lascelles has pointed out, their apparent confusions and irrelevances conceal the fact that information essential to the plot is being transmitted.[8]

Notes

1 S. Marcus, *Dickens from Pickwick to Dombey*, 1965, 80, 67.
2 P. Hobsbaum, 'The Critics and *Our Mutual Friend*', *Essays in Criticism*, 13, 1963, 233; K. Muir, 'Image and Structure in *Our Mutual Friend*', *Essays and Studies*, 1966, 98; R. C. Churchill, 'Dickens, Drama and Tradition', *Scrutiny*, 10, 1942, 361, 366.
3 J. Butt and K. Tillotson, *Dickens at Work*, 1957, 230–231.
4 R. L. Stevenson, *Letters*, ed S. Colvin, 1906, I, 220.
5 *Cf* A. Montagu, *The Anatomy of Swearing*, New York, 1967, 214–218. See also Smollett's Preface to *Roderick Random*.
6 P. Fairclough (ed), *Oliver Twist*, Harmondsworth, 1966, 28.
7 Crystal and Davy use the term 'common-core' to denote a type of utterance which is non-informative 'apart from the message being communicated' (*Investigating English Style*, 1969, 81–82). The whole of their discussion of 'stylistically significant characteristics' is interesting, though not all the questions they raise are relevant to fictional speech.
8 M. Lascelles, *Jane Austen and her Art*, 1939, 93–95. I have discussed Jane Austen's use of dialogue more fully in Ch 4 of my *The Language of Jane Austen* (Oxford, 1972).

Chapter 5

Some case-studies

The last two chapters of this book will be concerned less with general questions than with dialogue in context, as exemplified in specific novels of the past two hundred years. Chapter 6 will concentrate on the practice of a single novelist, Dickens; the present chapter offers a series of short case-studies based on individual works. Part of the problem of discussing speech in fiction is the need to maintain both a close-up and a long-range view: that is, to contrive to understand the nature of its presentation, and the mode of its operation, in relation to the verbal details of the text, without losing sight of the contribution of dialogue to the total effect of the novel. The two parts of this chapter examine the role of speech in, firstly, single chapters from three novels, and, secondly, three other novels considered in their entirety. Each method has, of course, its drawbacks: the first, like any application of 'practical criticism' or *lecture expliquée*, is apt to exaggerate the trivial and to raise the isolated instance to the status of a major feature of style; the second method, since novels are long and analyses must be short, suffers from an unavoidable superficiality. Nevertheless, there will be some value in pursuing discussion on the two levels of 'microcontext' and 'macrocontext', provided that we bear in mind that any individual feature needs to be related to the style of the novel as a whole, and that any general observations about a complex literary work need to be continually tested against specific instances.

The first group of examples, confined in each case to chapter-length, come from novels published at intervals of almost exactly one hundred years: Fielding's *Tom Jones*, Thackeray's *Vanity Fair*, and Graham Greene's *The Heart of the Matter*. The passages are too long to quote in full, but it is assumed that the interested reader will have no difficulty in locating them.

When Fielding turned to fiction he had behind him a successful career as a comic dramatist; and though critics have often been hypnotized by the author's own claim that *Tom Jones* (1749) should be viewed in terms of the classical epic, it retains at the same time abundant evidence of his theatrical training. Bk xv, Ch 5, is an excellent example of a scene conceived in terms of the stage and relying heavily on dialogue, and on theatrical elements verbally rendered, for its effectiveness. As the chapter opens, the reader has a sense of the curtain rising, with the heroine 'discovered' in a silent but eloquent situation:

> The clock has now struck seven, and poor Sophia, alone and melancholy, sat reading a tragedy.

She is soon joined by Lord Fellamar – the first of several entrances which will progressively complicate the action of this scene. What follows is essentially a passage of dramatic dialogue, with brief indications of movement ('Sophia started from her chair . . .') and facial expression ('with a look of inconceivable disdain'). In two ways, however, it differs from a dramatic script. One is the brief intrusion of the narrator's commentary to express approval of the heroine's attitude; the other is the bridging device, of the kind noted earlier in the discussion of direct speech, whereby a lengthy dialogue can be shortened by some such formula as 'My lord then made another and a longer speech of the same sort'. Indirect speech is used at one point, but enclosed in quotation marks according to Fielding's custom: '. . . concluded with a declaration, "That if he was master of the world, he would lay it at her feet" '.

The second phase of the scene begins when a voice is heard, 'off-stage', which the reader has no more difficulty in identifying than would the playhouse audience in a similar situation: the cry 'Where is she? D——n me, I'll unkennel her this instant', with its oath and its sporting metaphor, belongs unmistakably to Squire Western, who interrupts Fellamar at a crucial moment. Fielding's comment at this point seems to imply a regret for the more easily obtained dramatic effects of the writer for the stage: 'If the reader's imagination doth not assist me, I shall never be able to describe the situation of these two persons when Western came into the room.' In the ensuing dialogue, direct speech is less freely employed than in the earlier section, partly because the squire's language is of a kind that can be described but cannot with propriety be given verbatim ('he fell foul with his tongue in the most inveterate manner'), but also perhaps because Fielding does not want to lose speed. This does not prevent him, however, from giving one exchange which works in the same way as stage dialogue: by the direct implication of the speeches, that is, without any gloss or commentary by the author:

> "Let me intreat you, sir, to be a little more moderate," said the parson; "you frighten the young lady so, that you deprive her of all power of utterance."
>
> "Power of mine a——," answered the squire. "You take her part then, do you? A pretty parson, truly, to side with an undutiful child! Yes, yes, I will gee you a living with a pox. I'll gee un to the devil sooner."
>
> "I humbly crave your pardon," said the parson; "I assure your worship I meant no such matter."

The contrast between Western and the parson which would on the stage be reinforced by appearance, including costume, and by movement and gesture, is in the novel conveyed wholly at this point through the dialogue. Without excessive stylization, Fielding has created entirely distinct idiolects for the two characters: lexically, formal and homiletic language (*entreat, power of utterance*, etc) contrasts with colloquialisms and vulgarisms (*A pretty parson, with a pox*, etc); similarly, the parson's rounded periods throw into relief the exclamatory manner of the squire.

The situation is further complicated by the entry of Lady Bellaston, who not only represents another point of view and type of motivation, but brings into the scene another 'voice', that of the polite world:

> "Let me give him your hand, cousin," said the lady. "It is the fashion nowadays to dispense with time and long courtships."
>
> "Pugh!" said the squire, "what signifies time; won't they have time enough to court afterwards? People may court very well after they have been a-bed together."

The scene is therefore typical of what an earlier period would have called 'artificial comedy', successive entrances being exactly timed to provide the maximum effect. Dialogue and its accompaniments form the greater part of the chapter: description and comment are minimal. And this dialogue is of a kind that provides emphatic contrasts, as a stylistic equivalent to the bold characterization and the prominence of sudden, unexpected action. A few short quotations will illustrate this contrast in operation on the stylistic level:

> *Sophia:* If my death will make you happy, sir, . . . you will shortly be so.

Lady Bellaston: Indeed, Miss Western, . . . you injure your father; he
hath nothing in view but your interest in this match; and I and all
your friends must acknowledge the highest honour done to your
family in the proposal.

Squire Western: Don't think I am afraid of such a fellow as thee art!
because hast got a spit there dangling at thy side. Lay by your spit, and
I'll give thee enough of meddling with what doth not belong to thee.
I'll teach you to father-in-law me. I'll lick thy jacket.

Lord Fellamar: Though I have not the honour, sir, of being personally
known to you, yet, as I find I have the happiness to have my pro-
posals accepted, let me intercede, sir, in behalf of the young lady,
that she may not be more solicited at this time.

There is a sense in which, in such speeches as these, lexical and syntactical
features are made to correspond to qualities of moral character. The
formal syntax of Fellamar, remote from the normal structures of spontaneous speech, suggests the artificiality and unreliability of his behaviour
as well as his social status; at the other extreme, the blunt declarations of
Western, who prefers short sentences and has a marked distrust of subordinate clauses, are consistent with his impetuous manner and his in-
difference to canons of polite behaviour. His vocabulary relies heavily on
short, concrete words, in contrast to the fondness of the more morally
unsound characters for abstractions – Lady Bellaston's *interest* and *honour*
are typical – which are often (as in Fellamar's use of *honour*) embodiments
of moral ideas once meaningful but now drained of all but a token significance.[1] In contrast to all these, Sophia's sentence is elegant without being
elaborate, its structure appropriate to her refined but unaffected nature.
As in drama, therefore, it is possible to place the characters morally – as
well as socially and, where appropriate, regionally – through close attention to speech that is often praised for its realism, but in which nevertheless a highly conventional art can be seen at work.

A more obvious example of conventionalized speech for comparison
with the above can be found in the well-known chapter (v, 10) in which
the hero, somewhat the worse for drink, first soliloquizes in praise of
Sophia, vowing fidelity to her, and then, on the appearance of Molly
Seagrim, retires with the latter 'into the thickest part of the grove'. The
influence this time is less stage-comedy than mock-heroic, and Jones's
soliloquy, though highly entertaining, makes little pretence at plausibility. When the scene comes down to earth on the appearance of Molly,
and realistic dialogue would seem to be in place, Fielding deliberately

avoids it: 'Here ensued a parley, which, as I do not think myself obliged to relate it, I shall omit.' The subsequent appearance of Blifil and Thwackum again shows a marked tendency to play down the speech element, with indirect preferred to direct speech, as in 'Thwackum expressed some surprise at these sudden emotions, and asked the reason of them'. The chapter, which makes much less use of dialogue than a synopsis of its action would suggest as likely, is typical of a number which need to be remembered in assessing Fielding's debt to the theatre: it is responsible for some of his best writing, but does not blind him to the peculiar opportunities of fiction for varying the role of speech as well as the forms in which it can be presented.[2]

Perhaps the most dramatic chapter of *Vanity Fair* (1848), in conception if not in execution, is the fifty-third, in which Rawdon Crawley is first arrested for debt and then, after appealing unsuccessfully to his wife for help, released by another means; returning home, he finds Becky, who has told a sad tale of sickness, gorgeously attired and entertaining the wealthy Lord Steyne. What follows brings about the collapse of their marriage, and also marks the turning-point of Becky's fortunes as an adventuress. As this bald summary suggests, there is a good deal of narrative content for one short chapter, and considerable dramatic potential. What use does Thackeray make of speech, in relation to other elements, in his presentation of this material?

The chapter opens with the narrative voice firmly in command: the opening words ('Friend Rawdon . . .') reassert the confidential attitude to the reader, and the slightly condescending attitude to the characters, that are typical of this novel. The prose is ostentatiously 'literary' and whimsical in the manner of the familiar essayist: the sponging-house is 'Mr Moss's mansion', the Jewish servant has 'a head as ruddy as the rising morn', and the following fairly represents the arch and somewhat laboured style of this passage:

> The Colonel was not so depressed as some mortals would be, who, quitting a palace and a *placens uxor*, find themselves barred into a spunging-house; for, if the truth must be told, he had been a lodger at Mr Moss's establishment once or twice before.

The artificial diction (*mortals, palace*), the Latin tag, the euphemism of 'Mr Moss's establishment' and the elaborate sentence-structure make this essentially a written style, remote from the vocabulary or the rhythms of speech. When dialogue appears, it is the stock comic idiom of Mr Moss, with its Cockneyisms and its slang, and its indications of non-standard grammar and pronunciation. Such dialogue was very familiar to readers of light fiction, and could have been produced readily enough by any contributor to *Punch*:

> "I've got a Doctor of Diwinity upstairs, five gents in the coffee-room, and Mrs Moss has a tably-dy-hoty at half-past five . . ."

Rawdon's speech is deliberately played down: it suits Thackeray to maintain a light tone at this point, to contrast the more effectively with the latter part of his chapter. There follows an exchange of letters between Rawdon and Becky, their respective epistolary styles conveying, in an exaggerated form, the same kind of information about their natures as their speech does elsewhere. Rawdon's letter is brief, offhand, with bad spelling and free use of fashionable slang; Becky's fluent and plausible, sprinkled with French phrases and much verbal evidence of her affectation and insincerity.

After Rawdon's release, the narrative voice takes over until he is face to face with his wife and her lover. From this point the dialogue is in complete contrast to that of the earlier part of the chapter (including the two letters), and we hear the very accents of the melodramatic stage, accompanied by appropriate stage-directions: '"Before God, I am innocent!"' cries Becky, after uttering 'a faint scream' and smiling 'a horrid smile', and Rawdon abuses Steyne: '"You lie, you dog ! . . . You lie, you coward and villain!"' Finally Becky is left alone with her thoughts: 'What were her thoughts when he left her?' asks the narrator, but he makes little attempt to tell us, for after half-a-dozen lines the narrative voice again takes over to wind up the chapter.

The final and most dramatic portion of the chapter forms only about one-third of the whole: having engineered his big scene, Thackeray develops it less than one might have expected. Throughout the chapter, less use is made of dialogue than might have been anticipated from a summary of its action: on a line-count, less than one-third consists of speech, and both the serious dialogue and that in lighter vein tends to fall back on established idioms which owe more to literary and dramatic convention than to observation. Thackeray owed much to Fielding, but did not share his experience as a writer for the stage; though his dialogue is often lively, therefore, and more successful when comic or satiric than when (as in the chapter discussed) dramatic, he rarely achieves the quick-fire exchanges which are found in some of the best scenes of *Tom Jones*; and because the social range of *Vanity Fair* is narrower than Fielding's, the dialogue has less intrinsic vitality and variety. Technically, we find virtually no advance in methods of speech-presentation between the two authors; though, as previous examples have suggested, such contemporary and earlier novelists as Jane Austen and Dickens went a great deal further than Thackeray in extending the possibilities of fictional dialogue.

The brief opening chapter of Graham Greene's *The Heart of the Matter* (1948) may serve as a final chapter-length example of the place of dialogue in specific novels. Here, with characteristic economy, Greene contrives both to evoke his West African setting and to introduce some of his main characters within a few pages. The first two pages describe Wilson, 'almost intolerably lonely', sitting on the hotel balcony and looking down at the street below. With the arrival of Harris, there is a switch from narrative to dialogue, and the rest of the chapter (three more pages), apart from one paragraph and a few scattered 'stage-directions', resembles a dramatic script in its emphasis upon speech. These two sections of the chapter, the narrative and the dialogue, are differentiated by stylistic contrasts. In the first, the importance of the initial descriptions involves an extensive use of nominal groups which indicate with some precision the circumstantial quality of the exotic scene. Typical phrases are: 'the young negresses in dark-blue gym smocks', 'their wirespring hair', 'his very young moustache', 'brilliant afternoon dresses of blue and cerise', 'one bearded Indian in a turban'. This enumeration of items, with each noun accompanied by at least one epithet, is one of Greene's most obvious stylistic qualities; later in the same chapter he writes of 'a wound that would ache whenever certain things combined – the taste of gin at midday, the smell of flowers under a balcony, the clang of corrugated iron, an ugly bird flopping from perch to perch'. The listed phrases both make for economy and imply a logical incompleteness (since they are verbless) arising from the perception of experiences unrelated except insofar as they are part of an individual consciousness at a given moment. Atmosphere is created by the accumulation of sharply-observed and succinctly-expressed physical details, rather than by the development of a central idea. As the phrases quoted suggest, adjectives are frequent: there are more than thirty in this short passage, with much emphasis on colour here and throughout the chapter: 'bald pink knees', 'brown dog's eyes', 'a black man in a white panama'. In the dialogue adjectives are much rarer, and many of those which do appear belong to set phrases such as 'a high price', or are used in an intensive rather than a literal sense ('you old scoundrel', 'Eighteen bloody months') – a difference in frequency and function which would appear to reflect accurately the different natures of the written and the spoken (or literary and speech-based) language.

Both the narrative and the dialogue styles show a preference for short sentences, but there are structural contrasts between them. The former exhibits a tendency to avoid main verbs and subordinate clauses in favour of phrases, with a special fondness for the present participle: 'Sitting there, facing Bond Street, he had his face turned to the sea.' Greene's characteristic syntax in narrative and descriptive prose is seen in the following:

> he wore his moustache like a club tie – it was his highest common factor, but his eyes betrayed him – brown dog's eyes, a setter's eyes, pointing mournfully towards Bond Street.

He prefers, that is, coordination of clauses to subordination, and simple sentences paratactically arranged to either. Through parataxis – setting side by side, without connectives, phrases or sentences which would more usually be linked in some closer grammatical relationship – he achieves economy and emphasis, and also manages to suggest a narrative 'voice', since this is a common device of speech:

> he wore his moustache like a club tie / it was his highest common factor brown dog's eyes / a setter's eyes

One has the sense, at such points (marked / above), of the sentence not as a structural pattern foreseen by its writer from the opening but as developing, sometimes unexpectedly, and groping its way towards the adequate expression of meaning in a manner more readily associated with spontaneous speech than with the written word. 'A setter's eyes', for example, refines on the preceding phrase (which is nonetheless permitted to stand) in the same way that a speaker rejects an imprecise word for a more expressive one by pausing and then repeating the group of words with a slight stress on the changed element. To this extent the syntax of the narrative section has a speech-based quality. The dialogue itself draws on somewhat different aspects of informal speech.

One of the most obvious of these is Greene's use of brief utterances not necessarily forming sentences as the term is understood for the written language. In these three pages there occur thirty-five speeches, containing a total of eighty-two sentences, nearly three-quarters of which are of six words or less. It is as if tropical heat and the weariness of exile inhibit lengthy discourse. And the term 'sentence' is to be taken as covering such structures as

Why the bathroom?
The Syrians?
Rather.
Poor old Scobie.
Going home soon?

The dialogue is thus fast-moving but limited in subtlety – very much, indeed, what might be expected from two men who have no difficulty in placing each other socially or in finding common topics, but whose relationship has not yet had time to develop. It reveals, on broad lines, the different personalities of the two men, and provides necessary information concerning a third; but it does so dramatically and largely without supplementary comment. Thus it is different in function from the more descriptive and analytical manner of the omniscient narrator in the early part of the chapter, and the difference is mirrored in the respective styles of the two parts. Both stand in a perceptible relationship to speech: the narrative syntactically rather than lexically, the dialogue drawing on the observed qualities of a fairly predictable variety of speech, that of a readily identifiable social and educational group.

We turn next to brief consideration of the role of speech in three novels, each considered in its entirety.

STERNE: *Tristram Shandy*

In the eighteenth-century novel, the presentation of speech is found most readily at the level of dramatic dialogue – in, for example, the strongly theatrical scenes of *Tom Jones* which have already been referred to – and this legacy is inherited in the next century by Dickens, Thackeray, and others. The epistolary novel, superficially very different, can be seen as to an important extent a special case of this dramatic mode, so that the letters of Clarissa Harlowe often resemble the declaimed monologues of a tragic heroine. But there is another way in which the spoken language exerts its pressures upon fictional prose: in the usually one-sided 'dialogue' which takes place between author (or narrator) and reader. In Fielding, it is true, this relationship is public and formal, and the influence of speech-characteristics consequently very limited; but in *Tristram Shandy* (1760–67) the close confidentiality of Sterne's tone finds its appropriate vehicle of expression in a prose style often strongly modified by the features of spontaneous speech. The short opening chapter immediately suggests some of the roles that speech will play in this novel. At least four of these may be distinguished:

[1] The narrative voice – supposedly that of Tristram the hero, though clearly at many times close to that of the author. This is relaxed informal, consciously personal in tone: we can, indeed, find something very close to it in Sterne's letters, as in the following to Catherine Fourmantel, written in 1759, shortly before the publication of the first volumes of *Tristram Shandy*:

> My dear Kitty.
> If this Billet catches you in Bed, You are a lazy, sleepy little Slut – and I am a giddy foolish unthinking fellow for keeping You so late up – but this Sabbath is a day of rest – at the same time that it is a day of Sorrow – for I shall not see my dear Creature today – unless you meet me at Taylor's half an hour after twelve – but in this do as You like – . . . .

This recalls the comment in *Tristram Shandy* that 'Writing . . . is but a different name for conversation': not only does the direct address produce an intimacy of tone quite unlike that of most written prose, but the sentence quoted grows beneath the writer's pen in unplanned and unforeseen ways, moving forward in little lurches as a new idea, or a fresh aspect of one already stated, strikes his mind. An obvious symptom of this is the punctuation, rhetorical rather than logical, with Sterne's favourite and omnipresent use of the dash. The remoteness of such sentences from the normal literary prose of the period can be seen by comparing them with Sterne's style in writing to different correspondents with whom his relationship was more formal; thus he writes to the Bishop of Gloucester in the following year:

> Be assured, my lord, that willingly and knowingly I will give no offence to any mortal by anything which I think can look like the least violation either of decency or good manners; and yet, with all the caution of a heart void of offence or intention of giving it, I may find it very hard, in writing such a book as 'Tristram Shandy', to mutilate everything in it down to the prudish humour of every particular.

Sterne, that is to say, could handle both a Ciceronian and a speech-based style; for the narrative voice of his novel, he chooses the latter, as its opening sentence immediately makes clear:

> I wish either my father or my mother, or indeed both of them, as they were in duty both equally bound to it, had minded what they were about when they begot me . . .

The sentence continues for another 112 words before reaching its destination, by way of digressions and back-tracking: it thus offers in miniature a sample of both the stylistic quality and the narrative method of the novel. It is closer to the letter to Miss Fourmantel than to that to the Bishop of Gloucester; and closer to the opening of *Catcher in the Rye* than to that of *David Copperfield*. The phrase 'or indeed both of them', and the clause that depends upon it, create precisely the impression of a mind in the process of thinking as the sentence unrolls, and accommodating its impressions instantly in a highly flexible and adaptable syntax.

[2] The second sentence of the chapter opens with the words 'Believe me, good folks . . .', and this is the first of some 350 direct appeals to the reader in the course of this novel. Whereas most novelists keep the reader at a distance, Sterne, like any good conversationalist, constantly seeks to bring his audience into the situation he is creating through language; and whereas most who address the reader (as Thackeray and George Eliot do frequently) assume a homogeneous audience, Sterne appeals at different times to the whole or a part, and to different sections within it: it is, as Watt has pointed out, 'the jester's trick of dividing some of his audience into different groups, and mobilizing the rest of the audience for and against them'.[3] We thus find in the novel an extensive range of forms of address: *Sir, dear Sir, Madam, My Lord, Sir Critick, Gentle Critick,* and particular individuals such as *Jenny, Eugenius, dear Yorick, my dear friend Garrick,* etc. With these different appeals go a variety of tones: the address to the typical female reader, *Madam,* for instance, is often archly flirtatious or slyly indecent. The directness is reinforced by the use of the second person pronouns ('Well, you may take my word . . .' in the first chapter) and by imperatives: 'Lay down the book . . .', 'Imagine to yourself . . .' At one point Sterne goes so far as to invite the reader to sit down on a pile of the published volumes – surely an exceptional instance of calculated reader-involvement.

[3] The narrator is unavoidably a monologuist; but at times Sterne seems to wish to overcome the barriers of time and place between himself and his audience, and to develop their relationship in dialogue. This he does by hypothesizing the reactions to some of his direct appeals of a given section of his audience, and expressing the resulting argument through conversation:

– How could you, Madam, be so inattentive in reading the last chapter? I told you in it, *That my mother was not a papist.* – Papist! You told me no such thing, Sir. Madam, . . . I told you as plain, at least, as words, by direct inference, could tell you such a thing. – Then, Sir, I must have missed a page. – No, Madam, – you have not missed a word. – Then I was asleep, Sir . . . (I, xx)

and so on, leading to a request that the reader reperuse the previous chapter.

[4] Not least important are the dialogues between characters, typified in the opening chapter by Mrs Shandy's untimely question ('Pray my dear . . . have you not forgot to wind up the clock?') and her husband's impatient reply. These dialogues are notable for embodying two important characteristics of spontaneous speech: from the user's point of view, its random and disorganized quality, and from the listener's, its inherent capacity for being misunderstood. Locke writes of 'a train of Ideas, which constantly succeed one another', and the speech with which Sterne endows his characters is an exemplification of Lockean psychology. Whereas most earlier novelists' dialogue represents an orderly exchange of information and ideas between one character and another for the reader's benefit, Sterne is less concerned with developing action than with rendering the quality of individual moments of consciousness and with showing language to be a very imperfect medium for communication. Thus, when Uncle Toby reads the letter bringing news of Bobby's death, the effect is very different from most scenes of the kind:

– he's gone! said my uncle Toby. – Where – Who? cried my father. – My nephew, said my uncle Toby. – What – without leave – without money – without governor? cried my father in amazement. No: – he is dead, my dear brother, quoth my uncle Toby. (v, ii)

The elliptical quality of this exchange (most of the speeches dispense with main verbs) brings it close to informal speech and also ensures abundant opportunities for misunderstanding. The tendency to error is reinforced by the fixed ideas or 'hobby-horses' of the leading characters, who interpret what they hear in terms of their own prejudices. Uncle Toby, whose mind is dominated by the concepts and language of military science, interprets a dead metaphor such as *point-blank* literally and jumps from auxiliary verbs to military auxiliaries; his propensity is of course exaggerated for comic purposes, but the trait is a universal one for which the nature of language itself must be held partly responsible.

As quotations have shown, Sterne, who goes further than any other novelist in exploiting graphological and typographical devices and the whole nature of the book as a physical object, avoids the quotation marks which distinguish sharply between speech and non-speech, preferring instead to merge one with the other. This is logical enough, if one regards the narrator's dialogue with the reader, like the characters' conversations among themselves, as essentially implying a speech situation. In both the all-purpose dash is used to break up sentence-units and to control the reader's response more emphatically than conventional punctuation:

> – I am half distracted, captain Shandy, said Mrs Wadman, holding up her cambrick handkerchief to her left eye, as she approached the door of my Uncle Toby's sentry-box – a mote – or sand – or something – I know not what, has got into this eye of mine – do look at it – it is not in the white – (VIII, xxiv)

As often, speech is accompanied by stylized gesture (the most famous example of this occurs when Trim drops his hat to the floor in reflecting on human mortality). Smoothness of construction is deliberately eschewed: reading the above passage, the reader finds himself moving along in a series of short spurts, in a way which mimes the coy hesitations of the Widow Wadman and the impromptu nature of her speech. The narrative voice can use the same technique, as in describing the dying Le Fever: '– the pulse fluttered – stopped – went on – throbbed – stopped again – moved – stopped – shall I go on? – No.' Rather than organizing experience and seeking to present a coherent overall picture of it, syntax at such times works dramatically by reproducing symbolically the experience and its accompanying emotions: the sentence stops and moves on again like the sick man's pulse, and the reader receives the impression that, so far from the outcome being foreseen from the start, anything might happen at any moment, medically and syntactically. We have not the straight line of normal expository prose but the changes of direction, the variations in speed, above all the unpredictable quality of ordinary speech. Sterne's achievement is not only to write brilliant comic dialogue but to utilize features of speech in the novel as a whole, and thus to attain a familiarity and flexibility of tone which had not before been found in the English novel.

GEORGE ELIOT: *Adam Bede*

A hundred years after *Tristram Shandy*, *Adam Bede* (1859) typifies the concern of nearly all the major Victorian novelists to present the drama of individual lives in their social context. In this early novel, George Eliot confines her scope to the provincial and rural community remembered from her own youthful experiences; nevertheless there are enough differences in status between the characters (as well as differences of other kinds) to guarantee variety in the dialogue. And we find in George Eliot a quality shared by Scott and Hardy: while much of the narrative is conveyed in a verbose and often ponderous style, some of the dialogue passages are strikingly different. As soon, that is, as she forgets to speak in her own voice and allows her characters to speak for themselves – as soon as the intellectual with an articulated didactic purpose gives way to the woman recalling, nostalgically but accurately, ways of life (including modes of speech) observed in her childhood and youth – the prose quickens to a new life. In the second chapter of the novel, Mr Carson the innkeeper points out his own superiority to the locals in, among other respects, the matter of speech:

"... I'm not this countryman, you may tell by my tongue, sir. They're curious talkers i' this country, sir; the gentry's hard work to hunderstand 'em. I was brought hup among the gentry, sir, an' got the turn o' their tongue when I was a bye. Why, what do you think the folks here says for 'hevn't you?' – the gentry, you know, says, 'hevn't you' – well, the people about here says 'hanna yey'. It's what they call the dileck as is spoke hereabout, sir. That's what I've heard Squire Donnithorne say many a time; it's the dileck, says he."

The delicate irony of this passage reveals the standpoint of one who is able to regard 'the folks here' and the 'gentry', as well as phenomena like the innkeeper, with equal detachment: one has only to consider the more elaborate and exaggerated way in which Dickens might at the same time have treated the same material to appreciate George Eliot's concern for accuracy. As it turns out, the 'gentry', the users of 'dileck', and the contrasts and conflicts between them, are to form a major theme of the novel. The central character, Adam, alternates between regional and standard speech (see p 72 above): at home he is apt to slip back into the language of his childhood under the infectious influence of his mother's strongly non-standard speech, but for the most part his dialogue is more consistent with his heroic status. For George Eliot, that is, as for Hardy later, regional speech is largely reserved for comic, pathetic or sentimental-nostalgic purposes. For more heroic or dramatic effects, standard speech is a *sine qua non*.

The inconsistency within the dialogue given to Adam Bede is well illustrated by the major scene (Chs 27–28) in which he taxes Arthur

Donnithorne, the upper-class seducer, with his behaviour towards Hetty. The social gulf between the two men, normally obvious enough, is closed as Adam's anger rises, and his speech undergoes a corresponding change. One index of this is the disappearance of the form of address 'sir', used at the beginning of the scene but not later when Adam speaks under the pressure of feeling. By the time they come to blows, Adam speaks to Arthur as man to man, and their speech is virtually indistinguishable:

"I never meant to injure you," said Arthur . . . "I didn't know you loved her."

"But you've made her love *you*," said Adam. "You're a double-faced man – I'll never believe a word you say again."

"Go away, I tell you," said Arthur angrily, "or we shall both repent."

"No," said Adam, with a convulsed voice, "I swear I won't go away without fighting you. Do you want provoking any more? I tell you you're a coward and a scoundrel, and I despise you."

Having expressed his moral indignation by knocking Arthur out, however, Adam's consciousness of social differences returns: '"Do you feel any pain, sir?"', and there are more than a dozen further 'sirs' in the ensuing dialogue. With this return of respect for one's natural betters comes a partial return of lower-class and dialectal forms, notably the elision in such words as *o' th'house, t'Hetty, y'aren't*. Lexically, the more formal and even theatrical language of the climax (*scoundrel, despise*, etc) yields to a homely diction more appropriate to Adam's background and standing:

"Y'aren't going away for ever; and if you leave her behind with a notion in her head o' your feeling about her the same as she feels about you, she'll be hankering after you, and the mischief may get worse. It may be a smart to her now, but it'll save her pain i' th' end."

Adam's speech, therefore, displays a quality to which that of many Victorian lower-class heroines and heroes is prone: its approximation to the standard language varies in relation to the intensity and solemnity of the moment.

Humble life is the main focus of the novelist's interest in *Adam Bede*: she refers at one point to 'the faithful representing of commonplace things', and the influence of the literary ideals of Wordsworth and Scott is perceptible. As exemplified by Adam and Seth, or the Poyser family, it

is seen not merely as a historically and sociologically interesting phenomenon, but as the embodiment of certain unpretentious but solid virtues: honesty, integrity, kindness, loyalty. Homely speech, it follows, is
necessarily something more than a curiosity or a source of comedy or
local colour: it is rather an expression of traditional wisdom which is
shown as absent from the more orthodox but emotionally sterile language of the upper-class characters. Moreover, George Eliot's rustic dialogue
is not all of one kind. It has already been suggested that Mrs Bede's speech
is much more broadly dialectal than that of Adam; it is also differentiated
from that of another dialect speaker, Mrs Poyser, as the following extracts
show:

> "Come, then," said Lisbeth, "but donna thee ate the taters for Adam
> 'ull happen ate 'em if I leave 'em stannin'. He loves a bit o' taters an'
> gravy. But he's been so sore an' angered, he wouldn't ate 'em, for all
> I'd putten 'em by o'purpose for him. . . ."

> "Why, you might think you war come to a dead-house," said
> Mrs Poyser . . . ; "they're all i' the meadow; but Martin's sure to be in
> afore long, for they're leaving the hay cocked to-night, ready for
> carrying first thing to-morrow. I've been forced t' have Nancy in,
> upo' 'count as Hetty must gether the red currants to-night; the fruit
> allays ripens so contrary, just when every hand's wanted. An' there's
> no trustin' the children to gether it, for they put more into their own
> mouths nor into the basket; you might as well set the wasps to gether
> the fruit."

The differences spring partly from differences of social status – the farmer's
wife is far enough from pretensions to gentility not to be ashamed of
her country speech, but is markedly superior to the poor widow; they
also reflect a contrast in temperament and intelligence, the self-pitying
complaints of the one finding a mode of speech quite different from the
tolerant good humour of the other. Mrs Poyser's declarative and digres-
sive manner avoids monotony by the concreteness of her language and
the vigorous humour and good sense of the epigrams to which she is
addicted, which are in themselves a reflection of a wisdom derived from
first-hand experience of country life. In this respect she contrasts with the
Methodist Dinah, whose abstract nouns and parallelism of syntax suggest, in their echoing of biblical and theological texts, an unworldly and
humourless cast of mind.

HENRY GREEN: *Doting*

Henry Green's *Doting* (1952) is a novel in which dialogue has a more prominent place than in the work of any other novelist with the exception of Ivy Compton-Burnett. There is little narrative or descriptive writing, and virtually no comment or analysis by the narrator, who remains determinedly detached from the world of the novel and equally unwilling to enter into any relationship with the reader: he is, in fact, a recorder rather than (as are most novelists) a commentator or interpreter, and apparently as impersonal as any mechanical recording device. Action in this novel is minimal: what we find in its place is a series of dialogues involving half-a-dozen characters in groups of different sizes and combinations. There are no chapter-divisions, and it is the shaping of these dialogues, in themselves and in relation to each other, that provides the formal patterning of the novel. Although most of the characters work for their living, we learn nothing of what they do; the main character, Arthur Middleton, is a successful business man, but we are never told the nature of his business. There are vague references to 'the office' and 'the ministry', but it is their private lives, and their social and emotional entanglements as worked out in conversation, that form the substance of the fictional interest. For these characters talk incessantly, usually in the setting of some formal or semi-formal occasion such as a meal in a restaurant.

The talk itself is often commonplace in thought and trite in expression – designedly so, of course. On the other hand, the dialogues as presented in the novel have a formality of structure that reminds one of opera. The novel opens, for instance, with a quartet of voices over dinner, speaking now together, now in pairs; and it ends with another dinner (the end of the holidays which have begun as the book opened) at which the number of participants has grown to six, reflecting the complications of relationships with which the novel is concerned. Between these two occasions lies a series of duets, trios, and other groupings. The reader is thus in a God-like position, enjoyed by none of the characters, to compare X's conversation on a given topic with Y with the version he gives to Z, to relate what he has been reported as saying to Y with what he tells Z he has said to Y, and so forth: to detect, that is, the conscious and unconscious inconsistencies, retouchings of the truth, hypocrisies and evasions which are part of the nature of speech in its social function. He is also able to perceive ambiguities and to recognize concealed allusions and significant repetitions which may not be apparent to at any rate some of the participants. This gives these dialogues an interest of a rather special kind – an interest which is not localized but which comes from holding in one's mind, as one reads this short novel, a large number of separate conversations.

What is implicit in the above account is that Green's dialogue is very difficult to illustrate adequately by brief quotation. (In this respect, and in others, he differs from Ivy Compton-Burnett, whose dialogue offers an immediate aesthetic satisfaction and is apparently more substantial, richer in statement and suggestion, than Green's.) There are no purple patches or *tours de force*, no epigrams and little repartee. The following, like almost any other passage one might pick on, is typical:

"And did you make an appointment to meet Ann, once more?" the wife enquired, without looking at her husband.
"Of course not."
"Are you sure, Arthur?"
"Darling, what is this? Are you in one of your moods when you're about to claim second sight again?"
"I might be. Yes."
"Well, Diana, you're wrong, that's all."
"Am I? Because I might only be going to the nearest hotel, you know, instead of Scotland."
"Now really! What are you saying, dear?"
"And don't you forget it!"
"Yes, darling."
"That's better" she said in an approving tone. (*p* 163)

Green is far from generous in providing contextualizing information: after the revealing phrase 'without looking at her husband', the words of which the speeches are composed constitute the sole means of communication between author and reader until the reference to 'an approving tone' in the last sentence quoted. This places a burden on speech which it does not have to carry in real life, where meaning is supplemented, reinforced or qualified by gesture, facial expression, vocal tone, etc, or indeed in most novels. Nor does the language used seem to be of a quality that enables it to carry such a burden easily: Green uses for his mainly upper-middle-class characters a social dialect very limited in its resources: *wonderful* (often *rather wonderful*) is its all-purpose term of praise, displeasure is conveyed by *rotten* or *awful*, and *darling* is a universal and meaningless form of address. The action seems to be set in the post-war period, but the colloquial language used by the young as well as the middle-aged characters has the flavour of an earlier generation: references to a *cad* and *an utter ass* occur, for instance, on a single page (219). There is little differentiation between the speech of different characters. All of which may seem to imply severe limitations of scope and interest; and it is true that, beside that of the great nineteenth-century novelists, Green's dialogue offers little variety. Its interest, however, is to be found beneath the surface, in the process of discerning the unspoken hopes and fears, thoughts and motivations, to which the words uttered often act as a smokescreen. In the passage quoted, Arthur Middleton is anxious to repudiate suspicions of his intended misconduct during his wife's absence; she is anxious to make it clear that she is aware of his probable intentions and does not propose to tolerate his behaviour; but neither wishes to abandon the long-standing custom of domestic harmony and marital good terms. The conversation, therefore, is pulled in two directions: by a disruptive tendency towards accusation and self-defence, and by a stabilizing or at least pacifying tendency towards the preservation of at any rate the illusion of compatibility. The signals, varying in intensity at different points, by which a close relationship is implied are worth attention.

A. McIntosh has suggested that there are available to us various 'markers of involvement', linguistic devices by means of which we claim or stress a relationship with an interlocutor; some of the more obvious of these are the use of second person pronouns, the inclusive 'we', the imperative, and forms of address of different degrees of formality or informality (including names, titles, nicknames, and an extensive range of such locutions as 'my dear' and 'ladies and gentlemen').[4] The usage of nineteenth-century novelists reflects a society in which the appropriate forms were scrupulously observed by all who aspired to propriety; one result of this is that occasional departures from the norm can have a disproportionately dramatic effect to which present-day fiction can achieve no exact parallel. When a nineteenth-century heroine, for instance, uses her lover's Christian name (Amy Dorrit and Lizzie Hexam are cases in point), the moment has a special quality that the novelist writing in a more permissive society cannot easily imitate.[5] Green's use of forms of address is most commonly to make an ironic point: *darling*, for instance, becomes less a genuine endearment than an instant and unsupported claim to intimacy or an attempt to paste over the cracks of a disintegrating relationship. We see this in the passage quoted: the use of *Arthur* as the wife presses her point has the effect of aiming the question at him more directly and inescapably; his repeated *darling, Diana, dear, darling*, intended to be reassuring, is a symptom of his insecurity, and it is significant that his most emphatic

denial is accompanied by a use of her Christian name – the verbal equivalent of looking her straight in the eyes, as opposed to the vagueness of his
answered protest '"What are you saying, *dear*?"' The use of the second
person throughout also evinces an attempt (not entirely wholehearted) to
suggest a living relationship: such a phrase as 'one of *your* moods' could
hardly be used to a stranger.

As already indicated, Green's dialogue does not lend itself to quotation
or anthologizing; and this is one way of paying tribute, even if indirectly,
to its realism. As in life, the remarks made by his characters are rarely
memorable or striking in expression: often they fall back on cliché, or
understatement, or silence; but, viewed in their totality, his dialogues can
be seen to proceed from attitudes and relationships which are part of the
emotional fabric of the novel. He is not afraid of exhibiting linguistic
poverty where this is an accurate index of emotional dishonesty or spiri-
tual emptiness; though unavoidably limited in range, therefore, his work
is distinctive in quality and capable of conveying with some subtlety the
conscious and unconscious dishonesties of the eminently respectable.

Notes

1 *Cf* G. W. Hatfield, *Henry Fielding and the Language of Irony*, Chicago, 1968.
2 J. Butt, *Fielding*, 1959, has some useful brief comments on the dramatic element in
  Fielding's novels.
3 I. Watt, Introduction to the Riverside edition of *Tristram Shandy*, Boston, 1965,
  xxix. *Cf* also the same author's 'The Comic Syntax of *Tristram Shandy*' in *Studies in
  Criticism and Aesthetics, 1660–1800*, ed H. Anderson and J. S. Shea, Minneapolis,
  1967, 315–331.
4 A. McIntosh, 'Grammar and Style', *Durham University Journal*, 55, 1963, 120.
5 *Cf* N. Page, 'Forms of Address in Dickens', *The Dickensian*, 67, 1971, 16–20.

Chapter 6

Dickens and speech

In the preceding chapters, the novels of Dickens have provided a fertile source of material for illustration and discussion. His lifelong interest in the spoken language, manifested at many levels, was the product of both natural gifts and early training; and among novelists he is outstanding, perhaps unique, for the variety and effectiveness of his dialogue. It seems worthwhile, therefore, to devote a further chapter to a fuller consideration of some of the manifestations of his highly-developed speech-consciousness.

With some novelists, we can only speculate as to the relationship between their dialogue writing and their use and awareness of speech in daily life. The career of Dickens, on the other hand, is sufficiently well-documented for some significant elements to become apparent. Angus Wilson has observed that his 'greatest natural gift was his ear',[1] and the gift was one that was not long in being recognized by his contemporaries. Whilst they were generally content to ignore his style – and when they did not ignore it, were ready to attack it for its seeming disregard of the canons of grammatical correctness – reviewers of his early novels lavished praise on their dialogue, and especially on the presentation of lower-class speech. The *Edinburgh Review* pointed out in 1838 that 'All the characters are made to discourse in the appropriate language of their respective classes', adding that 'his plan is, not to describe his personages, but to make them speak and act . . .'. A few years later the *Athenaeum* referred to Sam Weller's 'flowers of slang', and the *Monthly Review* asked, 'What can be compared with [Mrs Gamp's] peculiar jargon?' As early as 1837, reviewing Dickens's first published writings, the *Quarterly* had heralded him as 'the first to turn to account the rich and varied stores of wit and humour discoverable among the lower classes of the Metropolis', and two years later the same influential magazine announced with a flourish, in a review of *Oliver Twist*, 'Boz is regius professor of slang'.

We can now see that this unusual skill in representing the spoken language was derived partly from what must have been a marked natural aptitude, and partly from early training of an unsystematic but valuable kind. Before he turned to writing, Dickens's experiences as a reporter and shorthand-writer – that is, as a professional recorder of speech – must have sharpened his already keen powers of aural observation and provided a sound basis of knowledge of certain varieties of speech such as the legal and the political. He spent some seven years as shorthand-reporter at Doctors' Commons and in the law courts (the Lord Chancellor's Court and the Old Bailey, as well as Bow Street and various other metropolitan police courts), and as journalist on the staff of the *Mirror of Parliament*, the *True Sun*, and the *Morning Chronicle*. As a parliamentary reporter he spent three sessions (1832–34) in the House of Commons, where his assignments included some powerful speeches by O'Connell and, possibly, the maiden speech of Gladstone. All these experiences helped to provide material for characters and scenes in the novels; but even more importantly, he acquired habits of visual and aural observation that were to persist long after he ceased to earn his living as a journalist. His heroic efforts to master Gurney's shorthand are recorded in some unmistakably autobiographical passages of *David Copperfield* (Chs 38, 43). Gurney's, a notoriously difficult system dating from the mid-eighteenth century and widely used for legal reporting, was not phonetically based; but the continual recording and transcription of actual speech, in which great importance was attached to accuracy, must have been a significant part of the apprenticeship of the future writer of dialogue. Dickens's skill in this direction seems to have been of no common order; and in a speech delivered towards the end of his life he recalled his time as a shorthand-reporter and declared an 'undying interest in this old calling'.[2]

If these experiences help to account for his acute powers of observation of speech habits and his capacity for reproducing them accurately, another early interest is relevant to the role accorded in the novels to speech, gesture and movement. This was his passionate interest in the theatre and his assiduous study, at first hand, of contemporary techniques of acting. 'As a child', we are told, 'he was a demon reciter as soon as he could steady himself on a table top', and what a recent biographer has referred to as a 'precocious gift for recitation and mimicry' extended throughout his life and became eventually an important, and lucrative, branch of his professional activity.[3] After he abandoned the idea of a career in the theatre, his enthusiasm for amateur dramatics absorbed much time and energy for many years, and his appearances in a variety of roles continued until 1857.

Contemporary accounts testify to his remarkable powers of assuming the speech and manner of the character he was playing: one witness described his voice as possessing 'great flexibility', another praised the 'consummate effect' of his articulation in the role of Shallow.[4] As an established author, his interest in holding an audience through the spoken medium – an audience whose response was more immediate and gratifying than that of the usually invisible audience of the writer – found two further outlets. He was much in demand as a public speaker, and 'was considered by a number of his contemporaries to be the best after-dinner speaker in England'.[5] In one of these speeches he remarked that 'every writer of fiction, though he may not adopt the dramatic form, writes in effect for the stage';[6] and he achieved a success which may fairly be described as unparalleled with his public readings from his own works, given at first (from 1853) for charity and subsequently (from 1858) for payment. He prepared at various times twenty-one readings – dramatic scripts adapted from his published writings – of which five were never delivered; and he gave altogether, in Britain and the USA, some 470 performances.[7] The relationship between these reading versions and the original texts on which they are based throws some interesting light on Dickens's awareness of the nature of the differences between the written and spoken media. Most of the reading versions are based on passages from the earlier novels, and comparison shows that the changes made, which involved heavy revision as well as extensive deletions, resulted in a tighter, more concentrated and more rhetorical use of language. In turn, there is every reason to believe that the written style of the later novels (from *A Tale of Two Cities*) bears signs of the influence of Dickens's experiments in oral presentation.

Consider, for example, the comic anecdote of the child who swallowed a necklace, originally in *The Pickwick Papers* and rewritten in 1861 as part of a reading titled *Mr Bob Sawyer's Party* which was to prove extremely popular. The following brief extracts are taken from, respectively, the earlier and the later versions:

Child's parents were poor people who lived in a court. Child's eldest sister bought a necklace; common necklace, made of large black wooden beads. Child, being fond of toys, cribbed the necklace, hid it, played with it, cut the string, and swallowed a bead . . .

Child's parents, poor people, lived in a court. Child's eldest sister bought a necklace, common necklace, large black wooden beads.

Child, being fond of toys, cribbed necklace, hid necklace, played with necklace, cut string of necklace, and swallowed a bead . . .

The omission from the reading version of inessential words (*were, who, made of, the*), combined with the reiteration of *necklace*, produces a more insistent rhythm: compare the metrical quality of

. . . cribbed the necklace, hid it, played with it, cut the string, . . .

and

. . . cribbed necklace, hid necklace, played with necklace, cut string of necklace, . . .

Furthermore, we have the testimony of an ear-witness (the American journalist, Kate Field) that Dickens employed a remarkably exaggerated range of intonation in reading this passage aloud.[8] It seems clear that Dickens's revisions were designed to enable him to exploit qualities of speech that the written language is not fully equipped to convey, but which would be undeniably effective on the public platform.

Dickens took particular pains over his last reading version, *Sikes and Nancy*: he wrote to W. H. Wills that in the week before the first performance he was engaged in 'polishing the Murder minutely every day'. A comparison between a short passage from the *Oliver Twist* of thirty years earlier and the corresponding passage in *Sikes and Nancy* will show the direction of some of these changes:

"No, sir, I do not," replied the girl, after a short struggle. "I am chained to my old life. I loathe and hate it now, but I cannot leave it. I must have gone too far to turn back – and yet I don't know, for if you had spoken to me so, some time ago, I should have laughed it off. But," she said, looking hastily round, "this fear comes over me again. I must go home."

"No, sir. I am chained to my old life. I loathe it and hate it, but I cannot leave it. When ladies as young and good, as happy and beautiful, as you, miss, give away your hearts, love will carry even you all lengths. When such as I, who have no certain roof but the coffin-lid, and no friend in sickness or death but the hospital-nurse, set our rotten hearts on any man, who can hope to cure us! This fear comes over me again. I must go home."

What is new in the later version is a bolder rhetoric of which the most obvious manifestation is the pattern of dramatic antitheses, the vivid particularity of *coffin-lid* and *hospital-nurse* contrasting favourably with the undistinguished diction of the original. The two sentences which are completely new have a quality that might loosely be described as theatrical; they also illustrate Dickens's increased fondness in his later style for marked patterning, including a strong element of repetition. The second, indeed, represents a carefully-modelled variation on the first:

| 1 'When ladies | as young and good, | |
| 2 'When such as I, | who have no certain roof but the coffin-lid, | |

| 1 as happy and beautiful, as you miss, | give away your hearts, | |
| 2 and no friend . . . hospital-nurse, | set our rotten hearts on any man, | |

1 love will carry even you all lengths.
2 who can hope to cure us?

The second sentence thus reproduces the main elements of the first, providing in each case a contrast between the middle-class girl and the wretched prostitute, until the final clause dramatically shows the resemblance they share.

The reading versions, then, show Dickens exploring a new area of the oral medium and devising in the process a style which was also to leave its mark on the late novels – a style which may be described as 'written to be read aloud' or 'written to be spoken'. This is not to overlook the fact that a strong oral element exists in the earlier work of Dickens, and in the work of other Victorian novelists: the habit of reading fiction aloud was, after all, a well-established one of which at least some authors must have been conscious as they wrote, and to speak of the narrator's 'voice' in these novels is something more than a figure of speech. But the later novels show, in an altogether more precise sense, stylistic qualities to the development of which the public readings, which occupied so much of his time and energy during those years, must have made an important if indirect contribution.

One of the most interesting features of Dickens's development over some thirty-five years, indeed, lies in the changing relationship between his dialogue and non-dialogue writing, and the changing role in his work of speech-based prose. This aspect of his development can be strikingly illustrated by comparing his first and last completed novels, *The Pickwick Papers* and *Our Mutual Friend*. A single chapter from each must serve, for present purposes, as a representative sample. Chapter 13 of *Pickwick* is the well-known account of the Eatanswill election. Slightly more than half

the chapter, on a line-count, consists of dialogue: but what is more significant is that this dialogue shows marked stylistic contrasts with the narrative and descriptive writing with which it is interspersed. This creates for
the novelist, with each switch to or from dialogue, the problem of making
a transition that is effective without being obtrusive; and it must be
admitted that Dickens does not at this stage always contrive the gear-
change with perfect smoothness. The introduction of Mr Pott is a case in
point: after a preliminary description of this new character, we read that
'The new-comer was introduced to Mr Pickwick as Mr Pott, the editor
of the Eatanswill Gazette. After a few preliminary remarks, Mr Pott
turned round to Mr Pickwick, and said with solemnity . . .' – and a passage of dialogue ensues. Those 'few preliminary remarks' are a somewhat
clumsy device to accomplish the change of mode from narrative to
speech: one senses the young novelist moving rather uncertainly from one
element to the next, and his technique is no further advanced in this
respect than that of Fielding or Smollett. The stylistic contrasts between
narrative and dialogue are also very evident. The chapter in question
opens as follows:

> We will frankly acknowledge, that up to the period of our being
> first immersed in the voluminous papers of the Pickwick Club, we
> had never heard of Eatanswill; we will with equal candour admit, that
> we have in vain searched for proof of the actual existence of such a place
> at the present day.

This is both a parody of a contemporary journalistic and editorial style
(in continuation of the vein in which the novel opens), and a fair sample
of much of the arch and wordy humour of this and many other passages;
one has the suspicion that Dickens, faced with the problem of covering a
prescribed number of sheets, is profiting from the expansive qualities of
this style at the same time as he ridicules it. For he is, in his narrative
capacity at least, still heavily committed to the formal structures of the early
nineteenth-century sentence – the staple of Scott's novels and Macaulay's
essays, as well as of the journalistic prose of *Blackwood's* and the *Quarterly*.
This is, in other words, essentially *written* prose, with its own traditional
patterns of arrangement and subordination: a fit instrument for logical
discourse, but hardly adapted to convey either delicate and transitory
feelings or a sense of the spontaneously dramatic. More damagingly, he
relies on journalistic cliché to an extent that cannot be accounted for
entirely in terms of parody: apart from the four or five examples in the
sentence quoted, we find in the same paragraph 'anxious desire', 'emi-

nently remarkable', 'hazard a guess', and others. Hardly a noun appears without its (usually predictable) accompanying epithet, and many of the expressions used add little or nothing to the meaning. One of Dickens's mannerisms at this stage is to use two words instead of one: thus we have 'note and statement', 'utmost and most mighty', 'disputes and high words', 'foresight and sagacity', etc. At many points the creative impulse seems to have given place to the necessity of filling a column, and the sense becomes diffused throughout a mass of verbiage.

The dialogue, in contrast, is often admirably brisk and economical:

"Fine, fresh, hearty fellows they seem," said Mr Pickwick, glancing from the window.

"Wery fresh," replied Sam; "me, and the two waiters at the Peacock, has been a pumpin' over the independent woters as supped there last night."

"Pumping over independent voters!" exlaimed Mr Pickwick.

"Yes," said his attendant, "every man slept vere he fell down; we dragged 'em out, one by one, this mornin', and put 'em under the pump, and they're in reg'lar fine order, now. Shillin' a head the committee paid for that 'ere job."

"Can such things be!" exclaimed the astonished Mr Pickwick.

No wonder contemporary readers singled out the dialogue of *Pickwick* for special praise. Lexically, the narrative style (like much prose of its period) is often stiff with Latinisms: the opening paragraph of the novel contains, among other examples, *illumines, obscurity, immortal, assiduity, multifarious*. Against this setting, Sam Weller's colloquialisms, his frequent use of slang (often glossed for his employer's benefit), and his folkidioms, all rendered more vivid by indications of dialect pronunciation, acquire a bonus of vigour and come as a welcome relief. The syntax of his sentences also possesses a rhythmic quality that is missing from most of the novel's prose – the rhythms of speech rather than of written prose:

"Shillin' a head the committee paid for that 'ere job."

One can imagine the longer, flabbier sentence that would have carried a similar meaning in a narrative context. It is the dialogue which still reads aloud best and which remains in the memory.

From *Pickwick* to *Our Mutual Friend* is a leap of thirty years and an advance in style and technique comparable to that from *Love's Labour's Lost* to *The Tempest*. These years saw not only a prodigious output of fiction and journalism but also, as has been briefly indicated, much energy expended on acting, public speaking, and (most relevantly to the present theme) reading from his own work. It would have been extraordinary, in a man of Dickens's aural receptiveness, if the experience of carefully preparing and rehearsing, and repeatedly delivering, these dramatic scripts over a period of years had not resulted in perceptible changes in his written style. In fact the influence is profound and pervasive. It can to some extent be exemplified from the second chapter of *Our Mutual Friend*, though no text brief enough to be discussed here can represent its full importance: only a reading of the novels of the last eleven years of Dickens's life can do that.

The first thing one notes about the 'oral' style of *Our Mutual Friend* is the quality of the narrative voice, so much more flexible and astringently individual than the ponderous editorial manner of *Pickwick*. It is a voice that, rather than being modelled on written prose, seeks to imitate the emphatic rhythms and repetitions of speech – not, to be more precise, spontaneous or informal speech, but a heightened and often emotional rhetoric:

> Mr and Mrs Veneering were bran-new people in a bran-new house in a bran-new quarter of London. Everything about the Veneerings was spick-and-span new. All their furniture was new, all their friends were new, all their servants were new, their plate was new, their carriage was new, their harness was new, their horses were new, their pictures were new, they themselves were new, they were as newly-married as was lawfully compatible with their having a bran-new baby, and if they had set up a great-grandfather, he would have come home in matting from the Pantechnicon, without a scratch upon him, French polished to the crown of his head.

To set this chapter-opening beside the one already quoted from *Pickwick* is to see at once the radical reorientation of Dickens's style which must, in part at least, have been wrought by his experiments in oral delivery. The long sentence now seeks its effect not through the logical hierarchy of main and subordinate clauses in a complex structure, but by the cumulative and repetitive coordination of similarly-patterned units. The word *new* and its derivatives occurs fifteen times in a dozen lines, and in addition to these repetitions we find the recurrence of syntactical patterns: three clauses on the model of 'All their x was/were new' are followed by five on the model of 'their x was new', the sentence gathering momentum and rhythmic insistence as it proceeds:

> their plate was new,
> their carriage was new,
> their harness was new,
> their horses were new, . . .

The railway, which has rendered obsolete the coaches and horses of Mr
Pickwick's world, and which figured dramatically in the history of the
manuscript of *Our Mutual Friend* (see Dickens's *Postscript*), seems to have
lent its rhythms to the novel which opens 'In these times of ours', as it
did to Tennyson's poetry. In the process, the traditional sentence has been
to a significant extent rejected; for the example quoted is not an isolated
one, but typical of this late style. (Compare the introduction of Bradley
Headstone in Chapter 18: the words *decent* and (in various forms) *mechanical* occur seven and six times respectively in a short passage. Compare
also, for an example in the dialogue, Headstone's speech to Lizzie in
Chapter 15, already quoted (*p* 103 above).
Dickens's notes for this chapter include the following:

> Bradley Headstone's love
> "Love could draw me to fire –
> water –
> Gallows –
> what not!"

which seems to suggest that his conception of the speech started with the
anaphoric structure and its implicit rhythm, and then moved on to fill in
the details later.[9]) The grotesque, dehumanized image of the newly-pur-
chased great-grandfather represents another element which became, in the
later novels, of increasing importance: the use of metaphor and symbol,
allying these novels to poetic drama more closely than to the mainstream
of Victorian fiction. One of the most interesting unwritten books on
Dickens would be a study of the growth and function of the poetic
element in his work. Furthermore, the attitude to language itself is now
highly self-conscious and critical: whereas the *Pickwick* style relies heavily
on cliché, formulaic language and merely conventional speech is now the
target of satire:

> "Let me," says the large man . . . "have the pleasure of presenting
> Mrs Podsnap to her host. She will be" – in his fatal freshness he seems
> to find perpetual verdure and eternal youth in the phrase – "she will be
> so glad of the opportunity, I am sure!"

In the same chapter, the paragraph (too long to quote) beginning 'The great looking-glass above the sideboard...' is especially worth attention. Anaphora is used here to give pattern and unity to the description of a variegated scene: 'reflects' in the opening sentence is repeated ten times, nine of these repetitions serving to open a sentence of which the subject ('looking-glass') is omitted. This gives the paragraph something of the tone of a sardonic inventory, with the initial 'Reflects' as a synonym for 'Item' – appropriately so, since Dickens's descriptions again have a dehumanizing effect upon his characters, reducing most of them to a catalogue of features, mannerisms and personal impedimenta. The style has, too, the telegraphic succinctness of an auctioneer's catalogue: Mrs Podsnap, for instance, is evoked in these terms:

> Reflects Mrs Podsnap: fine woman for Professor Owen, quantity of bone, neck, and nostrils like a rocking-horse, hard features, majestic head-dress in which Podsnap has hung golden offerings.

In *Pickwick*, Jingle's speech, which has much in common with the above, was offered as a unique eccentricity aimed at a comic effect. In the later novel, the Jingle style has become a valid and not exclusively comic narrative medium which achieves force and directness by discarding such inessential verbal elements as articles and prepositions.

The dialogue of this chapter is highly diversified, ranging from the brilliantly witty social comedy of Mortimer and Eugene (a remarkable anticipation of Wilde) and the fantastic idiosyncrasy of Lady Tippins (a survival of the earlier manner), to the stylized anonymous chorus of minor guests:

> Then the four Buffers, taking heart of grace all four at once, say:
> "Deeply interested!"
> "Quite excited!"
> "Dramatic!"
> "Man from Nowhere, perhaps!"

But the role of speech in this new style extends far beyond the dialogue, of course. The stylistic contrast between dialogue and non-dialogue elements which was noted in *Pickwick* is greatly lessened: lexical and syntactic features which might earlier have been found in the dialogue but were excluded from the more formal prose of the narrative passages are now apt to turn up in any sentence of the novel, for the narrative style is itself permeated by the influence of speech – not so much spontaneous, informal discourse as the more elaborate kind of rhetoric which

Dickens knew from long and (in every sense) rewarding experience was capable of moving an audience. One by-product of this is that the some-times awkward transitions, as in *Pickwick*, involved in switching from narrative to dialogue or vice-versa have disappeared, since the more versatile narrative style can now accommodate larger or smaller frag-ments of dialogue without changing its own nature. These transitions from one element to another are eased by the frequent use, in the novels from *Bleak House* onwards, of free indirect speech.

Dialogue, then, can be seen in a changing relationship to other fictional elements in the course of Dickens's career. But at any stage the reader's response to dialogue is an important part of the experience of reading a Dickens novel, and common experience, for what it is worth, suggests also that these are the passages which tend to linger in the memory. The *Oxford Dictionary of Quotations*, to make a simple test, mentioning Dickens as among the half-dozen most frequently quoted writers in English, lists 262 extracts from his writings, at least 80 per cent of which are from dialogue passages. It is not only the major characters who emerge vividly in this way, though naturally the more extended roles exhibit a fuller and richer development. 'Q' pointed out that Mr F's Aunt in *Little Dorrit* 'left her unforgettable mark on the world in less than two hundred words',[10] and an even briefer existence is enjoyed by the waiter in the third chapter of the same novel, whose highly distinctive idiolect is ex-hibited in just twenty-six words. Minute analysis of character or mental state is not Dickens's forte, but what is beyond admiration is his skill in creating and in 'fixing', through language, a sense of humanity in action: men and women not being but doing and, very often, *saying*. As Percy Lubbock wrote half a century ago, 'He is happier in placing a character there before us, as the man or woman talked and behaved in a certain hour, on a certain spot, than in reflecting a long impression of their manner of living';[11] and this sense of here-and-now is largely conveyed by speech and its concomitants, by the apparently spontaneous give-and-take of language springing from dramatic situation and revealing character. Since this is the essence of the Dickensian method, it is worth considering how far he may have conceived character and incident in terms of speech in the initial planning of the novel. In this connection the working notes made for the later novels have for the most part survived to provide some interesting evidence.

Again and again, these demonstrate his habit of setting down the germ of an idea, later to be given fuller treatment, as a vivid fragment of speech. Thus, the plans for the fifth number of *David Copperfield* contain the phrase 'Miss Betsey – "Janet! Donkies!"', and *Hard Times* carries the following note: 'Mr Gradgrind. Facts and Figures. "Teach these children nothing but facts. Nothing but facts."' Other examples are legion. The chapter on 'Hints for books written and unwritten' in Forster's *Life* also cites several instances of Dickens's habit of noting 'a bit of . . . dialogue' or 'some oddity of speech' in the *Book of Memoranda* he kept from 1855. His constant alertness to the variety and expressiveness of everyday speech thus became an important contributory element in the conception of new fictional projects. Speech seems to have been as central to the author's production of a novel as it is to the reader's response: they are 'dramatic' novels in more than a merely vague or general sense, and it is surely significant that many of them were promptly and repeatedly adapted for the stage (for instance, seventeen different versions of *The Cricket on the Hearth* were produced in London within a month of its publication), and have, more recently, achieved another kind of success in the cinema and on radio and television. We have, from one of the novelist's daughters, a graphic little account which suggests that the process of composition may have partaken of the nature of a theatrical performance:

> . . . he suddenly jumped from his chair and rushed to a mirror which hung near, and in which I could see the reflection of some extra-ordinary facial contortions which he was making. He returned rapidly to his desk, wrote furiously for a few moments, and then went again to the mirror. The facial pantomime was resumed, and then . . . he began talking rapidly in a low voice. Ceasing this soon, however, he returned once more to his desk, where he remained silent writing until luncheon time.
> [Mamie Dickens, *My Father as I Recall him*, New York, 1898, 49–50]

That reference to his 'talking rapidly in a low voice' suggests the close-ness of much of his dialogue to speech, at least to dramatic speech.

An excellent and omnipresent example of his habit of conceiving character in dramatic terms is to be found in his use of the linguistic or other mannerism, the *tic* of language, tone, gesture or facial expression, which marks so many of his creations throughout the novels. No doubt the circumstances of serial publication, which placed a premium on quick identification of a character and easy recognition on subsequent appear-ances even after a lapse of weeks or months, helped to turn it into a major feature of his technique. The literary influence of the Jonsonian comedy of humours, especially as mediated through the Smollettian novel, must also have made a contribution: we know that Dickens was an enthusiastic actor in *Every Man in his Humour*, and Smollett's name heads the list of the hero's (and the author's) childhood reading in the fourth chapter of *David Copperfield*. Probably another important influence was that of the actor Charles Mathews the elder, who between 1818 and 1833 presented a series of one-man shows in which he played a large number of parts, distinguishing the various characters largely by speech differences – eccentric verbal tags, dialect, professional jargon, and so forth. Dickens saw Mathews towards the end of the veteran actor's career, and threw himself into a close study of his comic techniques; he later wrote to Forster that he went 'always to see Mathews whenever he played'. In another letter he writes of his early ambition to go on the stage: 'I believed I had a strong perception of character and oddity, and a natural power of reproducing in my own person what I observed in others'. It is this kind of perception, and a developing skill in expressing it, that is behind many of his most celebrated creations. Contemporary readers were struck, not always favourably, by his fondness for the identifying mannerism: a reviewer in 1859 predicted ironically that in future novels he might go so far as to 'have one character identified by his eye-brows, another by his nostrils, and another by his toe-nails'. It would certainly not be difficult to compile a very long list of characters associated with some favourite word or phrase or other verbal mannerism. For the moment, it will be enough to recall such well-known instances as Wemmick's 'portable property', Jarndyce's 'East Wind', Jerry Cruncher's 'honest tradesman', and Stephen Blackpool's 'All a muddle'. All these examples offer a tiny but significant clue to the nature and role of the character concerned. Others serve a mainly comic purpose, on the sound principle (confirmed by generations of music-hall and radio comedians) that a word or phrase unremarkable enough in itself will earn an increment of comic response on each reappearance. Tedium is avoided by not necessarily repeating the catch-phrase intact, a process of variation-within-repetition often combining the simple effectiveness of mechanically repetitive comedy with an element of the unexpected. Of this kind are Mantalini's variations on his favourite oath (*demd, demdest, demmit, demnebly*) and the terms of address, more extravagant as the novel proceeds, used to his wife. Nor is the labelling confined to the repetition of a word or phrase. It may consist in a feature of syntax (as with Jingle's telegraphic style, Joe Gargery's tortuous sentences, and Flora Finching's unpunctuated ramblings) or a peculiarity of pronunciation (as with Uriah Heep's *umble*, Mr Sleary's lispings, and the Wellers' interchange of *v* and *w*).

As in the theatre, speech is reinforced by such extralinguistic concomitants as movement, gesture and facial expression; and just as the style of acting favoured in the nineteenth century tended towards ample and unambiguous external tokens of a character's inner feelings, so Dickens tends to supplement dialogue with contextualizing information of this kind which, by frequent repetition, joins the class of identifying mannerisms. The 'stage-directions' which often accompany dialogue are full of visual equivalents of the catch-phrase, and many of these today strike a hollow note and remind us that gesture, like language, has its archaic and obsolete forms. But the devilish grimaces of Quilp and Blandois, or the villainous Ralph Nickleby (like Heathcliff) 'literally gnashing his teeth', would not have seemed outrageous to readers brought up on the conventions of the Victorian melodramatic stage. Contemporary elocution manuals stressed the importance of gesture, and a review in *The Times* of Dickens's own performance in *The Frozen Deep* praised 'the language of his eyes and facial muscles'. In the public readings, his copies were carefully marked with marginal notes where gesture was called for, and he paid close attention to stage-effect: 'He used a very light table covered with velvet without any drapery, that gesture, as well as facial expression, might be fully displayed'. Justin McCarthy put on record that, as a public speaker, Dickens gave 'additional force and meaning to what he said' by the use of 'his wonderfully expressive hands'; and there is evidence too that he made unusually frequent use of gesture in private conversation.[12] There are innumerable parallels to all this in the novels. One thinks of Pecksniff warming his hands before the fire, Uriah Heep pointing with his 'long, lank, skeleton hand', Gradgrind 'squarely pointing with his square forefinger', Turveydrop waving his gloves and Captain Cuttle his hook, Joe Gargery (like Beckett's Vladimir) fiddling with his hat; there is even a short essay on Bucket's forefinger in Chapter 53 of *Bleak House*. Few novelists have gone as far as Dickens in reinforcing the expressiveness of dialogue with descriptions of movement and gesture, and thus providing a visual counterpart to the oral element in his fiction.

Similarly, within the dialogue itself we find repeatedly a greater amount of linguistic information made available to the reader than most novelists provide – information which assists in the imaginative reconstruction of the variety of speech in question. As an actor and a skilled performer on the human voice, Dickens must have been more conscious than most novelists of the infinite subtleties of which speech is capable and, correspondingly, of what is inevitably lost in setting down speech in written form. If, as seems very likely, much of his dialogue was dramatically conceived, and mentally or actually acted out in the process of composition, we can expect to find frequent signs of the writer's struggle with his largely intractable medium; and in fact we do often have the sense of Dickens wrestling with the conventions of written prose in order to convey some faint suggestion of what the written language cannot by its nature adequately represent. It is surely revealing that he was, in correcting proofs, prepared to go to considerable pains to take a stand on minor questions of punctuation and typography. He seems, indeed, to have been unusually sensitive to the physical appearance of the written word, if his autobiographical heroes may be allowed to speak for him: we read of David Copperfield learning the alphabet ('the easy good-nature of O and Q and S . . . '. etc) and of Pip forming an idea of the father he has never known from the shape of the letters on his tombstone; and in one of his speeches he recalls early reading lessons:

> I distinctly remember praying for the printer as my greatest enemy. I never now see a row of large, black, fat, staring Roman capitals, but this reminiscence rises up before me.

In his novels he shows an unusual fastidiousness in the use of punctuation, which is often scrupulously revised in subsequent editions; and as an editor he firmly modified his contributors' punctuation in accordance with his own notions of what was desirable. His punctuation is often dramatic and rhetorical rather than logical, and editors who modernize it to avoid disconcerting the reader with unfamiliar usages do so at the expense of a certain loss of expressiveness. He will often vary normal conventions to obtain a special effect, as when Peggotty talks to David, in short breathless bursts, through a keyhole:

> "Davy, dear. If I ain't been azackly as intimate with you. Lately, as I used to be. It ain't because I don't love you. Just as well and more, my pretty poppet. It's because I thought it better for you. And for some-one else besides."

A whole range of phonological qualities is suggested by the skilful deploying of punctuation devices: hyphenation suggests an abnormal placing of stresses by American speakers (*con-cluded, lo-ca-tion*); capitalization and italicization are used to indicate emphasis (HEEP's name is given thus thirty-three times in Micawber's speech of denunciation); and punctuation, and even spacing, can disappear entirely to suggest an unbroken flow of speech or an intoxicated slurring of words. References to punctuation are also used, figuratively as it were, in the comment that accompanies dialogue, as when we are told that a witness 'has a good deal to say, chiefly in parenthesis and without punctuation'. A longer example will show how punctuation variants, combined with orthographic variants, can be orchestrated to suggest an idiolect of marked eccentricity: the speaker is the negro landlord of a Liverpool public-house, who is calling the figures for a dance. (As well as indications within the dialogue, Dickens adds explanatory notes to the effect that the speaker 'occasionally addressed himself parenthetically', and that 'When he was very loud, I use capitals'.)

"Now den! Hoy! ONE. Right and left. (Put a steam on, gib 'um powder.) LA-dies' chail. BAL-loon say. Lemonade! TWO. AD-warnse and go back (gib 'ell a break-down, shake it out o' yerselbs, keep a movil). SWING-corners, BAL-loon say, and Lemonade! (Hoy!) THREE. GENT come for'ard with a lady and go back, hoppersite come for'ard and do what yer can. (Aeiohoy!) BAL-loon say, and leetle lemonade (Dat hair nigger by 'um fireplace 'hind a' time, shake it out o'yerselbs, gib 'ell a breakdown.) . . ."

['Poor Mercantile Jack', *The Uncommercial Traveller*]

At such times, the conventions of the written language, for all their undeniable limitations and imperfections, operate with something resembling the effect of a crude system of musical notation; and at least once Dickens went so far as to employ the musical stave to record the absurdly exaggerated intonation of parliamentary orators:

And why, why, above all, in either house of Parliament must the English language be set to music – bad and conventional beyond any parallel on earth – and delivered, in a manner barely expressible to the eye as follows:

		night
	to	
Sir when I came do	this house	
o		
o		
wn to		

ters
___

Minis

ty's
___

I found Her   jes
___

___

___

Ma

Is Parliament included in the Common Prayer-book under the de-
nomination of "quires and places where they sing"?

[*Household Words*, 28 June 1851]

Dickens realized that phonological features are indeed 'barely expressible
to the eye', but that did not prevent him from stretching the resources of
the written language to express as much as was possible, and more than any
other English novelist. Perhaps his early and rigorous training in shorthand
had given him a special interest in systems of representing speech through
symbols; certainly there can be no doubt that a writer who takes such pains
to convey as much information about oral qualities as the written medium
can accommodate will also demand of his readers that they either read
aloud, or at least take pains to 'hear' inwardly, what he has written.

Having made certain points in general terms, it will be as well to turn
next to specific texts embodying – as, indeed, any text by Dickens is
likely to do – the presentation of speech in various forms and varieties. I
follow here the method of the previous chapter, and consider first a
limited portion of material which, in this case, provides evidence of
Dickens's response to specific stimuli in the language situation in which
for a time he found himself, turning secondly to discussion of a single
novel in as many of its aspects as space will permit.

Some idea of Dickens's responsiveness to the spoken language as part
of his social environment may be gained by considering a well-documented episode in his life which left its imprint on two of his books. His
first trip to America (1842) has been described by Steven Marcus as 'a six-
months' voyage into the English language',[13] and certainly the differences
between the British and American varieties of English seem to have struck
him with a force with which, in our own age of multifarious trans-
atlantic influences, it would be hard to find a parallel. He was not, of
course, the first in the field: a decade before his visit Mrs Frances Trollope

had published her *Domestic Manners of the Americans*, which was widely popular. Dickens knew Mrs Trollope and had possibly read her book, which quotes a number of examples of American speech and comments shrewdly on aspects of usage. Perhaps he had also come across the work of other commentators on the American scene, such as Thomas Hamilton's *Men and Manners in America* and Harriet Martineau's *Society in America*, both published in the eighteen-thirties. But what is so striking about *American Notes* and the relevant chapters of *Martin Chuzzlewit* is the evidence they provide about Dickens's habitual receptiveness to the endless varieties and oddities of speech. A passing reference in a letter to his wife (dated 15 April 1842) suggests that he not only observed speech behaviour but was also interested in seeking to account for its characteristics: he commented that 'All the women who have been bred in Slave States speak more or less like Negroes, from having been constantly in their childhood with black nurses'.

Some of his impressions are recorded in *American Notes* (1842), an early chapter of which describes a misunderstanding based on lexical confusion in one of his first encounters with American speech on its native soil: a waiter's reply to his order 'Right away!' (*ie*, immediately) is misunderstood as meaning 'in another room'; and later chapters record his puzzlement at the conversational use of *yes* to express a variety of possible attitudes, as well as the suggestive fact that 'whenever an Englishman would cry 'All right!' an American cries, 'Go ahead!' which is somewhat expressive of the national character of the two countries.' Phonological as well as lexical differences are noted, either by orthographic means without further comment (*eg, airth* for *earth*) or by explicit comment, as in the reference to 'route (always pronounced rout)' and the observation that 'the word prairie is variously pronounced *paraaer, parearer,* and *paroarer*'. Such notes constitute the raw material from which fictional dialogue can be constructed; and *American Notes* was quickly followed by a novel which made considerable humorous and satiric capital out of eccentricities of this kind. In the seven chapters of *Martin Chuzzlewit* (1843–4) which relate the hero's American adventures, the dialogue makes an important contribution to the impressions of rawness and oddity that Dickens wished to create in his picture of frontier society. There are many instances of orthographic variants suggesting non-standard pronunciation (*dooel* for *duel, air* for *are*, etc) and of modifications to the normal form of English words (*disputating*); but even more prominent are variations in stress, indicated by capitalization, hyphenation, italicization, the use of diacritics, or some combination of these methods. It is the unfamiliar *rhythms* of the spoken language which seem to have impressed themselves upon Dickens with particular force: one of the earliest reactions attributed to Martin upon disembarking in New York is expressed in the following comment on the manner of speech of his interlocutor in the first conversation he holds on American soil:

> ... his manner of saying it .. was odd enough, for he emphasized all the small words and syllables in his discourse, and left the others to take care of themselves ... (Ch 16)

In the chapters which follow, Dickens presents a series of characters who exhibit the extravagant rhetoric of the American language – as, that is, he chose to represent it fictionally, which may of course bear only a limited relationship to what he had heard. Three such characters will suffice as examples. The colloquial idioms of Mrs Hominy are at times too much for Martin, whose amused puzzlement, not unmingled with a sense of superiority, may perhaps reflect the attitude of his creator to some of the linguistic phenomena he encountered:

> "Pray, sir!" said Mrs Hominy, "where do you hail from?"
> "I am afraid I am dull of comprehension," said Martin, "being extremely tired; but upon my word I don't understand you."
> Mrs Hominy shook her head with a melancholy smile that said, not inexpressively, "They corrupt even the language in that old country!" and added then ... "Where was you rose?"
> "Oh!" said Martin, "I was born in Kent."

In the speech of Mr Hannibal Chollop (Ch 33), the windy rhetoric of popular pamphleteering and political oratory are satirized; and in the following chapter Mr Elijah Pogram offers an even more debased example of cliché-ridden rhetoric:

> "Our fellow-countryman is a model of a man, quite fresh from Natur's mould! ... He is a true-born child of this free hemisphere! Verdant as the mountains of our country; bright and flowing as our mineral Licks; unspiled by withering conventionalities as air our broad and boundless Perearers! ..."

The corrupt poeticisms of the passage, which continues in similar vein, are evident; and at this point one detects a relationship between the presentation of American speech and the central theme of the novel which suggests that the former is not merely a *jeu d'esprit*. Pogram resembles Pecksniff in that the pretentious hollowness of his speech is an outward token of moral shortcomings: speech is no longer merely a fascinating and entertaining external which provides infinite scope for the exercise of human absurdity, but a symptom of character. Dickens's comment on American society, therefore, is made not only through the narrated experiences and reflections of his hero and through direct authorial intervention, but also more indirectly through the various modes of speech, and the postures adopted by speakers.

While there is no such thing as a 'typical' Dickens novel, in the sense of one exemplifying all aspects of his many-faceted art, *Bleak House* has stronger claims than most to be considered representative. Chronologically, it stands almost precisely at the mid-point of his career; artistically, it belongs to a stage of development in which the quality of brilliant improvisation characterizing the early novels has largely given way to a mature control and deliberateness of purpose, without any of the loss in vigour and inventiveness that has been found in some of the later work. We may ask of it, as of any novel, two comprehensive questions: what is the importance of the role of dialogue? and what stylistic relationship exists between the dialogue and non-dialogue elements? Let us consider these in order.

The part played by dialogue as distinct from other varieties of prose or modes of presentation can be assessed either scientifically (by, for example, a line-count, or some other statistical method of arriving at a proportion) or impressionistically (by the reader's subjective recollections, involving a conscious or unconscious comparison between this and other novels). What is striking, however, and surely not irrelevant, is the extent to which Dickens himself conceived character and incident in terms of speech. The evidence of his working notes has already been briefly alluded to; for *Bleak House* it is worth giving a fuller, though by no means exhaustive, list of quotations from these notes (the character or episode referred to is indicated in parenthesis):

1 "You're a brimstone chatterer." (Ch 21: Grandfather Smallweed to his wife)

2 "That there's the wale, the bonnet, and the gound" (Ch 22: Jo recalls his meeting with the disguised Lady Dedlock)

3 "My children, you shall always live with me" (Ch 23: Mr Turveydrop)

4 "Discipline must be maintained" (Ch 27: Mr Bagnet)

5 "She will try to make her way into the little room. Keep her out!" (Ch 31: Esther tries to protect Ada from the smallpox)

6 "I have brought the answer guardian" (Ch 44: Esther agrees to marry Jarndyce)

7 "Who will tell him?" (Ch 58: refers to Sir Leicester Dedlock, after his wife's flight)

8 "And it was my mother cold and dead" (Ch 59: Esther finds Lady Dedlock's corpse)

This very selective list is long enough to show that these notes serve different purposes.[14] Some indicate the central idea behind a character introduced for the first time, or a line of development in an established character; others fix in the writer's mind the germ of what will turn into a significant incident. Sometimes the words noted in these memoranda are given a prominent position in the final text: my seventh and eighth examples are the last words of their respective chapters; sometimes they undergo considerable modification or expansion; sometimes they appear, in various forms, many times, serving as identifying mannerisms (Smallweed's *brimstone* is a case in point) for the character in question. The important implication of such evidence, however, is that for Dickens speech was very often the starting-point for crucial elements in the story as well as for effective minor touches.

Turning to the finished novel, one would have no difficulty in compiling a long catalogue of scenes in which dialogue plays a vital part, from the legal speech of the opening scene in the Chancery court to the conversation between Esther and her husband on the final page. In only one of the sixty-seven chapters is dialogue virtually absent, and this (Ch 66) is a special case as being the final instalment of the third-person narrative and the traditional summary of life at Chesney Wold after the action of the novel is over. More useful than mere cataloguing, however, will be some analysis of the content of specific chapters from different portions of the novel.

Chapter 19 begins with an essay two pages long on Chancery Lane in the long vacation, in a style at times reminiscent – as is the theme – of the *Sketches by Boz* of nearly twenty years earlier. When attention is at length focused on the Snagsbys' drawing-room, however, where the Chadbands' arrival is expected, the treatment becomes more dramatic, and the scene is presented largely through dialogue. Snagsby and his wife, Chadband and his, Guster, Jo, Guppy, even the anonymous police constable, all have speaking parts, and few of even the briefest utterances could be transposed without incongruity from one to another. Some of these idiolects have been established in earlier chapters and need only to be recalled to the reader by the reappearance of familiar features (*eg*, Snagsby's uxorious and self-deprecating forms of address); others are here introduced for the first time. The range of devices used to individu-alize the various characters may be illustrated by comparing the speech of Jo the crossing-sweeper and Chadband, the popular preacher. Jo's language is thick with orthographic variants to indicate non-standard pronunciation (there are nearly forty – the count varies slightly according to which text is used – in a single speech); some indicate minor devia-tions from the standard pronunciation, such as the omission or modifica-tion of initial or final consonants (*'ere, crossin*), others represent a more radical divergence (*inkwhich* for *inquest*), whilst others still are con-ventional signals of lower-class speech rather than attempts to render a particular pronunciation (*ses, wos*). He also uses cant language fairly freely ('hooked it' for 'went away', 'drains' for 'drinks'), and a form of syntax which serves to express the limitations of his mental life:

> "They're wot's left . . . out of a sov-ring as wos give me by a lady in a wale as sed she wos a servant and as come to my crossin one night and asked to be showd this 'ere ouse and the ouse wot him as you giv the writin to died at, and the berrin-ground wot he's berrid in . . ."

Yet this too is largely conventional, for there is a control and consistency in Jo's sentences, in spite of their superficial eccentricity, which would hardly obtain in real life: very rarely does he lose his way in one of these long and circumstantial structures. Chadband's syntactical patterns are no less distinctive but have a literary rather than a popular origin, deriving from the Old Testament via the evangelical pulpit. His speech, in all its windy pretentiousness and hollow sham, is indeed the man. (It has been discussed more fully above, *p* 95.) It seems clear that, whereas Jo's speech draws on a generalized and largely conventionalized notion of lower-class idiom, Chadband's is a more specific parody of the speech of a small and easily identifiable group, which probably drew on a greater degree of observation of actual examples. Dickens's manuscript notes for Chap-ter 19 contain the following fragment which seems to suggest that Chadband's speech germinated from an initial catechistical pattern which developed in the finished text into full-blown parody:

> "Can we fly my friends? We cannot. And why can we not fly my friends?"

Considerable as is the intrinsic interest of such speech, however, the dialogue in this chapter is by no means merely ornamental and incidental, nor can it be dismissed as 'comic relief'. A speech such as Jo's account of the 'lady in a wale' is of importance in the unfolding of the plot, and Chadband's sermonizing, which contrasts so markedly with his failure to do anything practical for the wretched outcast before his eyes, relates to one of the central themes of the novel, the shirking of responsibility.

Chapter 48, which culminates in the murder of Tulkinghorn, uses dialogue somewhat differently. An opening passage descriptive of the London scene, and Lady Dedlock's part in the social season, is followed by three dialogues involving different combinations of characters and succeeding one another in the fashion of operatic items: a passage between Lady Dedlock and her maid, a quartet involving Sir Leicester and his wife, Tulkinghorn the lawyer and Rouncewell the ironmaster, and another duologue, this time between Lady Dedlock and the lawyer who holds her secret in his power. The dramatic tension rises steadily and reaches considerable intensity in the last of these. What follows is a passage of narrative and descriptive writing in which speech is carefully avoided, yet in which the silence itself becomes eloquent – both the taciturnity of the lawyer (who is soon to be silenced for ever) and the preternatural stillness of the night that is shattered by the report of a pistol. As Tulkinghorn walks home, 'He is in the confidence of the very bricks and mortar. The high chimney-stacks telegraph family secrets to him. Yet there is not a voice in a mile of them to whisper, "Don't go home!"' Contrasting elements are thus skilfully balanced: after so much talk, the effect of the crime committed without the uttering of a syllable by either murderer or victim is heightened. Yet, though the voices of the characters are silenced, their place is taken by the narrative voice, itself often (as in the lines just quoted) giving the impression of addressing the reader directly.

A final example confined to chapter-length may be that part of Esther's narrative (Ch 59) which ends with the discovery of Lady Dedlock's corpse. This originally constituted the final section of the eighteenth number, for which the manuscript memoranda include the note: 'Pursuit interest sustained throughout'. The chapter has a strong narrative element, its main interest lying in the quest which finds its conclusion in the burial-ground. In these circumstances, it might be expected that speech would have little place; but there are two ways in which the impression of an individual speaking voice is given. Esther's first-person style has something of the effect of a breathlessly-written journal, and thus partakes of a more informal style than is customary in narrative prose; and she contrives to incorporate in her narrative a letter from Lady Dedlock and the quoted speech of a number of other characters (Bucket, Woodcourt, Snagsby, Guster), so that the oral element is not extinguished and stylistic monotony is avoided.

The narrative method of this novel calls for further comment, especially in its relationship to speech and in the relationship of the two halves of the narrative to each other. Dickens employs two narrators who contribute, by alternating irregularly, in almost exactly equal proportions: the third-person omniscient narrator who opens the novel is quickly succeeded by Esther Summerson, who relates her first-person account as one who has witnessed a good deal of the action, and they continue to share the narrative task to the end. Esther is not, like Jane Eyre or David Copperfield, indisputably the protagonist of her story, and much critical energy has been spent on the question of her satisfactoriness as a character. What is less ambiguous is her effectiveness as an observer and recorder: a reviewer in the *Athenaeum* for 17 September 1853 found in her 'the immediate power of the daguerrotype in noting at once the minutest singularities of so many exceptional people', and her self-effacing nature, while it may not be the stuff of which heroines are made, qualifies her admirably as a historian of the splendours and miseries of others. Given this conception of her function, one of Dickens's initial tasks was to differentiate with sufficient sharpness between the alternating narrative styles. The most obvious differentiation is the consistent contrast in tenses (present for the omniscient narrator, past for Esther's portions) to reinforce the contrast of first- and third-person verbs in the two narratives. But the stylistic contrasts go a good deal further than this: Esther's style is evidently intended to strike the reader as simple, artless, even naive, with a pleasing informality of tone and a lack of any pretension to fine writing; the impersonal narrative, on the other hand, is more dramatic and emphatic in its effects, making free use of rhetorical devices and exploiting a wider range of linguistic resources. A glance at the openings of the two narratives (Chs 1 and 3) shows that the contrast operates at several levels. Esther's (Ch 3) shows signs of unusually heavy revision in manuscript, implying a conscious striving after specific effects of style. In a context which has been created by the highly original and experimental prose of the opening chapters, it exhibits a preference for the familiar, even the trite word, for coordination rather than subordination (she is especially fond of *and*), and for exclamations ('She was a good, good woman!' etc) which seem to belong to the spontaneous style of the letter or journal. Typical epithets (on the first page from Esther) are *clever, little, great, beautiful, dear,* compared with *implacable, elephantine, haggard, undistinguishable*, on the opening page of the novel. What this adds up to is that both styles have a relationship to speech, but to different spoken styles: Esther's shares certain features with informal conversation, the third-person narrative is closer to the language of the political platform and the stage.

Both narratives naturally incorporate a good deal of dialogue, but do so in rather different ways. Esther records direct speech, lightening her task by occasionally having recourse to indirect speech, and often adds her own modest comments as a gloss. The third-person narrative achieves a bolder effect by extensive use of free indirect speech. The coroner's inquest in Chapter 11 provides an early instance: beginning with direct speech, it quickly takes on a more experimental method:

> Mrs Piper pushed forward by Mrs Perkins. Mrs Piper sworn. Anastasia Piper, gentlemen. Married woman. Now, Mrs Piper – what have you got to say about this?
>
> Why, Mrs Piper has a good deal to say . . . but not much to tell. Mrs Piper lives in the court (which her husband is a cabinet-maker) . . . Has seen the Plaintive wexed and worrited by the children (for children they will ever be and you cannot expect them specially if of playful dispositions to be Methoozellers which you was not yourself). . . .

This achieves vividness in familiar ways, by its variant spellings, lexical confusions and non-standard grammar. More importantly, it achieves remarkable pace and concentration by its readiness to modify normal forms: by the omission of main verbs from the narrative, by leaving the questions asked to be inferred from the replies given, and by the use of free direct and free indirect speech. At times this can result in a strongly rhythmic prose:

> Says the Coroner, is that boy here? Says the beadle, no, sir, he is not here. Says the Coroner, go and fetch him then . .
>
> O! Here's the boy, gentlemen!
>
> Here he is, very muddy, very hoarse, very ragged . . .

and at the conclusion:

> Verdict accordingly. Accidental death. No doubt. Gentlemen, you are discharged. Good afternoon.

In such passages, with the absence of speaker-attribution and of the normal graphological indications of dialogue, speech and narrative merge into one another.

To return to an overall view of the novel, some reference must be made, though with unavoidable superficiality, to the range of speech-varieties deployed. None of the novels draws its characters from a wider *social* range than *Bleak House*, and speech contributes largely to under-lining their placing on the social scale, from the aristocratic Dedlocks to the outcast Jo. Between these extremes lies a highly diversified middle class, with its own hierarchies even in relation to the members of similar occupations: Snagsby the law-stationer, for instance, is in speech and every other way the social superior of Krook, another representative of 'trade'. Other characters deliberately confound the attempt to fit them into a social category: Turveydrop's speech is at odds with his situation in the dancing-school, and the bohemian Skimpole is genuinely classless. We are in fact offered an extensive view of mid-nineteenth-century England, with representatives of most of the main strata as well as others who remind us that every society has its misfits and every system of classification its exceptions. To a notable extent, different groups speak a language variety which is unintelligible to those at a distant point on the social spectrum; the best example of this is when Jo and Lady Dedlock come face to face in Chapter 16 (see *p* 82 above). Dickens's revisions tend to stress the slang element in Jo's speech; its contemporary effective-ness may be judged from the fact that it is substantially preserved, and even extended, in two dramas based on *Bleak House* and staged in the 1870s.[15]

Occupational varieties are also well represented, especially (and natu-rally, given the novel's starting-point as a satire on Chancery) by repre-sentatives of the law ranging from the Lord Chancellor, through pro-fessional lawyers such as Tulkinghorn, Kenge and Vholes (all carefully differentiated from each other), to those existing on the periphery of the legal world. But no account of social and occupational groupings should be allowed to obscure the fact that Dickens goes beyond a crude branding of group-membership and endows each member with a mode of speech peculiar to himself: of the Dedlock family, for example, each speaks not in a uniform upper-class idiom but with an unmistakable voice, and one could no more confuse Sir Leicester with Volumnia than with Jo. All this is to say that Dickens's endlessly fertile genius for individuation through speech is one of the most impressive qualities of this rich and varied novel.

S. Ullmann has written of Balzac that

In the *Comédie Humaine* he was faced with a linguistic problem on an unprecedented scale: to make each class, each group and profession speak in its own characteristic way, and even to individualize the major figures through their language. In this task he could never have succeeded had he not been, by inclination and experience, an acute observer of linguistic processes.[16]

No less may be claimed for Dickens, in all of whose novels dialogue is not only unusually varied but also unusually important in relation to other elements. Even in *A Tale of Two Cities*, which was begun (as Dickens wrote in a letter of August 1859) with the intention of 'creating characters true to nature, but whom the story should express more than they should express themselves by dialogue', the role of speech is by no means insignificant, from the nocturnal encounter on the Dover road in the second chapter to Carton's dialogue on the way to the guillotine in the last; and there may be some connection between this intention and the generally acknowledged fact that this is one of the least successful, as well as one of the less typical, of his books. But where Dickens is concerned, 'speech', as this chapter has tried to suggest, is by no means synonymous with 'dialogue', since especially in the later novels narrative style is seen to shed many of the characteristics of traditional written prose in favour of a style which is, notably in its syntax and rhythm, strongly colloquial. The epithet 'Dickensian' hardly carries very precise associations; but if one were to try to identify a characteristic by which Dickens could be seen to differ from other novelists of his time, his commitment to the spoken language, and to the attempt to render some of its richness and subtlety through the written word, has a strong claim for consideration.

Notes

1   A. Wilson, 'Charles Dickens: a Haunting', *Critical Quarterly*, 2, 1960, 104.
2   *The Speeches of Charles Dickens*, ed K. J. Fielding, 1960, 348. *Cf* also W. J. Carlton, *Charles Dickens, Shorthand Writer*, 1926.
3   M. Rosenberg, 'The Dramatist in Dickens', *Journal of English and Germanic Philology*, 59, 1960, 1; C. Hibbert, *The Making of Charles Dickens*, 1967, 23–24.
4   F. G. Kitton, *Dickensiana*, 1886, 40; T. E. Pemberton, *Charles Dickens and the Stage*, 1888, 108.
5   M. H. Miller, 'Charles Dickens at the English Charity Dinner', *Quarterly Journal of Speech*, 47, 1961, 143.
6   *Speeches*, 262.
7   See C. Kent, *Charles Dickens as a Reader*, 1872; G. Dolby, *Charles Dickens as I Knew Him*, 1885; J. D. Gordan, *Reading for Profit: the Other Career of Charles Dickens*, New York, 1958; P. Collins, 'Dickens' Public Readings: the Performer

and the Novelist', *Studies in the Novel*, 1, 1969, 118–132, and 'The Texts of Dickens' Readings', *Bulletin of the New York Public Library*, 74, 1970, 360–380.

8 K. Field, *Pen Photographs of Charles Dickens's Readings*, Boston, 1871, 97–99.

9 On Dickens's use of repetition, see S. Monod, 'Some Stylistic Devices in *A Tale of Two Cities*', in *Dickens the Craftsman*, ed R. D. Partlow, Jr, Carbondale, 1970, 165–186.

10 A. Quiller-Couch, *Charles Dickens and Other Victorians*, 1925, 28.

11 P. Lubbock, *The Craft of Fiction*, 1921, 216.

12 J. B. van Amerongen, *The Actor in Dickens*, 1926, 39; *Speeches*, xx; P. Collins, 'Dickens in Conversation', *The Dickensian*, 59, 1963, 154, *Cf* also T. Murphy, 'Interpretation in the Dickens Period', *Quarterly Journal of Speech*, 41, 1955, 243–245; R. L. Brannan, *Under the Management of Mr Charles Dickens*, Ithaca, 1966, 81–82.

13 S. Marcus, *Dickens from Pickwick to Dombey*, 1965, 219.

14 Dickens's number-plans for *Bleak House* are reprinted in full, with an explanatory note, in my edition of the novel (Harmondsworth, 1971), 936–952.

15 J. P. Simpson's *Lady Dedlock's Secret* was produced in 1874, and G. Lander's *Bleak House: or Poor Jo* two years later.

16 S. Ullmann, *Style in the French Novel*, Oxford, 1957, 90.

Further references

W. Axton, *Circle of Fire*, Kentucky, 1966.

G. L. Brook, *The Language of Dickens*, 1970.

E. Davis, *The Flint and the Flame*, New York, 1963.

R. B. Glenn, 'Linguistic Class-indicators in the Speech of Dickens' Characters', unpublished dissertation, Michigan, 1961.

R. L. P. Jackson, 'Language as a Means of Characterization in the Novels of Dickens', unpublished dissertation, Cambridge, 1968.

N. Page, 'Eccentric Speech in Dickens', *Critical Survey*, 4, 1969, 96–100.

L. Pound, 'The American Dialect of Charles Dickens', *American Speech*, 22, 1947, 124–130.

R. Quirk, *Charles Dickens and Appropriate Language*, Durham, 1959.

R. Quirk, 'Some Observations on the Language of Dickens', *A Review of English Literature*, 2, July 1961, 19–28.

H. Stone, 'Dickens and Interior Monologue', *Philological Quarterly*, 38, 1959, 52–65.

W. A. Ward, 'Language and Charles Dickens', *Listener*, 23 May 1963, 870–871, 874.

V. M. S. Wilson, 'Aspects of Dickens' Use of Conversation in the Novels', unpublished dissertation, King's College, London, 1955.

Discussion material

The following selection of material is designed to stimulate further thought, and in some cases practical analysis, in relation to topics dealt with in this book.

[I] SOME OBSERVATIONS ON DIALOGUE

a The dialogue is generally the most agreeable part of a novel; but it is so only so long as it tends in some way to the telling of the main story. It need not seem to be confined to that, but it should always have a tendency in that direction . . . The writer may tell much of his story in conversations, but he may do so by putting such words into the mouths of his personages as personages so situated would probably use. He is not allowed, for the sake of his tale, to make his characters give utterance to long speeches, such as are not customarily heard from men and women. The ordinary talk of ordinary people is carried on in short sharp expressive sentences, which very frequently are never completed, – the language of which even among educated people is often incorrect. The novel-writer in constructing his dialogue must so steer between absolute accuracy of language – which would give to his conversation an air of pedantry, and the slovenly inaccuracy of ordinary talkers, – which if closely followed would offend by an appearance of grimace, – as to produce upon the ear of his readers a sense of reality. If he be quite real he will seem to attempt to be funny. If he be quite correct he will seem to be unreal . . .

[Trollope, *Autobiography*, 1883]

b [The writer of dialogue] is synthesizing a 'spoken' language that will never be spoken. . . . He has to imagine all the circumstances, all the effects upon his characters, and at the same time has to give the impression of fluidity of utterance without on the one hand falling into the

profundities of formal, conventional prose, or on the other hand com-
mitting to paper the confusions and obscurities of actual speech.

[A. H. Smith and R. Quirk, 1955]

c Even a writer with a talent for capturing colloquial structures on paper
cannot forget that the primary function of his dialogue is to be the
vehicle for his plot.   [R. Quirk, 1955]

d Dialogue . . . consistently echoes the accepted speech of the day.

[I. A. Gordon, 1966]

e Every writer of fiction, though he may not adopt the dramatic form,
writes in effect for the stage.

[Dickens, *Speech for the Royal Theatrical Fund*, 1858]

f Dramatic dialogue remains a distinct type of language; it is not spoken
language written down.   [Halliday, McIntosh and Strevens, 1964]

g [Dramatic dialogue] constitutes a supreme idealization of life, for it
signifies a life which has a clear and unitary meaning, a direction, an
utterly purposive movement towards an end.   [E. Bentley, 1965]

h It has been known for some time that the 'spoken' word need not be
given *verbatim*, as it were, but that it can be presented with varying
degrees of directness or obliqueness.   [C. Jones, 1968]

i Neutrality is no good for the novelist. But if he accurately catches on
the printed page the West Indian tone of voice, he has to reckon with
the fact that what may sound insulting or ingratiating in one dialect
may signal something quite different to speakers of another dialect.

[R. B. Le Page, 1969]

[2] SOME EXAMPLES OF DIALOGUE IN FICTION, 1742–1966

a "Don't talk so soft, Albert Cockcroft," I said.
    You know, Gladys, I never use those Yorkshire expressions, I don't
like them; but I felt I had to be Yorkshire just that once.

[P. Bentley, *Tales of the West Riding*, 1965]

b "To begin wi'," I says, "a Yorkshire pudding is eaten by itsen and not
mixed up wi' meat and potaters, all in a mush. And it comes straight
out o' tooven," I says, "straight on to t'plate. No waiting," I says,
"or you'll spoil it. If you don't put it straight on to t'plate you might
as well go and sole your boots with it. And another thing," I says,
"you've got to have your oven hot, I do knaw that. Then if you've
mixed right and your oven's hot, pudding'll come out as light as a

feather, crisp and brarn, just a top and a bottom, you might say, wi'
none o' this custardy stuff in t'middle. Nah d'you see, Missis?" I
says ...   [J. B. Priestley, *The Good Companions*, 1929]

c As Hall stood there he heard his wife's voice coming out of the depth of
the cellar, with that rapid telescoping of the syllables and interrogative
cocking up of the final words to a high note, by which the West
Sussex villager is wont to indicate a brisk impatience. "Gearge! You
gart what a wand?"   [H. G. Wells, *The Invisible Man*, 1897]

d He was very sorry, he was deeply grieved; he couldn't say with what
unwillingness he came to prepare her for the intelligence of a very slight
accident. He entreated Mrs Dombey to compose herself. Upon his
sacred word of honour, there was no cause of alarm. But Mr Dombey –
Florence uttered a sudden cry. He did not look at her, but at Edith.
Edith composed and reassured her. *She* uttered no cry of distress. No,
no.
Mr Dombey had met with an accident in riding. His horse had
slipped, and he had been thrown.
Florence wildly exclaimed that he was badly hurt – that he was
killed!
No. Upon his honour, Mr Dombey, though stunned at first, was
soon recovered, and though certainly hurt was in no kind of danger ...
                                      [Dickens, *Dombey and Son*, 1847–8]

e The debilitated cousin holds that it's – sort of thing that's sure tapn
slongs votes – giv'n – Mob.
Debilitated cousin thinks – Country's going – DAYVLE – steeple-
chase pace.   [Dickens, *Bleak House*, 1852–3]

f The lawyer likewise made several very pretty jests, without departing
from his profession. He said, "If Joseph and the lady were alone, he
would be more capable of making a *conveyance* to her, as his *affairs*
were not *fettered* with any *incumbrance*; he'd warrant he soon suffered a
recovery by a writ of *entry*, which was the proper way to create *heirs
in tail* ..."   [Fielding, *Joseph Andrews*, 1742]

g I said to the Minister: "You must have spent a fortune today."
He smiled at the glass of cold beer in his hand and said:
"You call this spend? You never see some thing, my brother. I no de
keep anini for my self, na so so troway. If some person come to you and
say 'I wan' make you Minister' make you run like blazes comot. Na
true word I tell you. To God who made me."
                                      [C. Achebe, *A Man of the People*, 1966]

h ". . . what is the use of my being charming, if it is to end in my being dull and not minding anything? Is that what marriage always comes to?"

"No, child, certainly not. Marriage is the only happy state for a woman, as I trust you will prove."

"I will not put up with it if it is not a happy state. I am determined to be happy – at least not to go on muddling away my life as other people do, being and doing nothing remarkable. I have made up my mind not to let other people interfere with me as they have done . . ."

"I am sure I have never crossed you, Gwendolen."

"You often want me to do what I don't like."

"You mean, to give Alice lessons?"

"Yes, and I have done it because you asked me. But I don't see why I should, else. It bores me to death, she is so slow. She has no ear for music, or languages, or anything else. It would be much better for her to be ignorant, mamma: it is her *role*, she would do it well."

"That is a hard thing to say of your sister, Gwendolen . . ."

"I don't see why it is hard to call things by their right names, and put them in their proper places . . ."   [G. Eliot, *Daniel Deronda*, 1876]

i He clasped his hands on his stomach again. "I remained on board that – that – my memory is going (*s'en va*). Ah! Patt-nà.* *C'est bien ça*. Patt-nà. *Merci*. It is droll how one forgets. I stayed on that ship thirty hours . . ."
     [Conrad, *Lord Jim*, 1900]

f "In the ordinary way," said Holy Joe, "he'll come up afore the beak to-morrow morning and be remanded for a day or two, p'r'aps a week, p'r'aps a fortnight. I dunno. Then he'll come up again, and p'r'aps be remanded again. Then he'll come up once more and they'll either give him the drag or a sixer –"

"Easy on wi' the slang," said Maddie. "Talk English."

"Three months or six months, I mean, o' course."
     [E. Pugh, *Mother-Sister*, 1900]

k He finished blowing his nose, pushed the handkerchief back up his sleeve, and, using without facetious implication a then popular catchword, said: "How's your father?"

"All right."

"And your mother?"

"Very well."

---

* Patna: the name of a ship.

"Good," said Uncle Giles, as if it were a relief to him personally that my parents were well, even when the rest of the world might feel differently on the same matter.

There was a pause. I asked how his own health had been, at which he laughed scornfully.

"Oh, me," he said. "I've been about the same. Not growing any younger. Trouble with the old duodenal. I rather wanted to get hold of your father about signing some papers. Is he still in Paris? I suppose so."

"That bit of the Conference is finished."

"Where is he?"

"London."

"On leave?"

"Yes."   [Anthony Powell, *A Question of Upbringing*, 1951]

1 "And how are you?" said Peter Walsh, positively trembling; taking both her hands; kissing both her hands. She's grown older, he thought, sitting down. I shan't tell her anything about it, he thought, for she's grown older. . . .

Exactly the same, thought Clarissa; the same queer look; the same check suit; a little out of the straight his face is, a little thinner, dryer, perhaps, but he looks well, and just the same.

"How heavenly it is to see you again!" she exclaimed. . . .

He had only reached town last night, he said; would have to go down into the country at once; and how was everything, how was everybody – Richard? Elizabeth? . . .

"Richard's very well. Richard's at a Committee," said Clarissa.

And she opened her scissors, and said, did he mind her just finishing what she was doing to her dress, for they had a party that night?

"Which I shan't ask you to," she said. "My dear Peter!" she said.

But it was delicious to hear her say that – my dear Peter! Indeed, it was all so delicious – the silver, the chairs; all so delicious!

Why wouldn't she ask him to her party? he asked. . . .

[Virginia Woolf, *Mrs Dalloway*, 1925]

Index

References in the notes are indicated by *n* after a page-number